# THE
# ANOINTING

## Preceding the Messianic Age

McDougal & Associates
Servants of Christ and Stewards of the
Mysteries of God

# THE
# ANOINTING
### Preceding the Messianic Age

by

## LUCILLE
## PARKERSON

Unless otherwise noted, all scripture quotations are from the *Holy Bible,
English Standard Version*, copyright © 2001 by Crossway Bibles, a
division of Good News Publisher. Quotations marked AMPC are from
the *Amplified Bible*, Classic Edition, copyright © 1954, 1958, 1987 by
The Lockman Foundation. Quotations marked GNT are from the *Good
News Translation*, Second Edition, copyright © 1992 by American Bible
Society. Quotations marked KJV are from The Holy Bible, King James
Version, public domain. Quotations marked MSG are from *The Message:
The Bible in Contemporary English*, copyright © 1993, 1994, 1995, 1996,
2000, 2001, 2002 by Eugene H. Peterson. Quotations marked NIV are
from *The Holy Bible, New International Version*, copyright © 1973, 1978,
1984, 2010, 2011, by International Bible Society. Quotations marked NLT
are from *The Holy Bible, New Living Translation*, copyright © 1996 by
Tyndale House Publishers, Inc. Greek and Hebrew definitions are derived
from Abingdon's *Strong's Exhaustive Concordance of the Bible,* copyright
1890 by James Strong.

Cover design by projectluz.com

Published by:

**McDougal & Associates**
**18896 Greenwell Springs Road**
**Greenwell Springs, LA 70739**
**www.thepublishedword.com**

ISBN 978-0-99602177-7
Printed on demand in the U.S., the U.K. and Australia
For worldwide distribution

# Contents

# Acknowledgments

I dedicate this book and acknowledge my immense gratitude to my best friends and spiritual mentors, Christ Jesus and the Holy Spirit. Following a holy visitation, the Lord God placed in me the desire to write this memoir and sent me helpers and confirmations. I am forever grateful for His great love and sacrifice. It was His love that drew me to Him as a young girl and the demonstration of His love that kept me believing and serving Him.

I am forever grateful to the tremendous blessing He has given me in my dear husband, Rich. Through forty-five years of marriage, Rich has continuously demonstrated his faithfulness, love, kindness, and generosity. During the many years I was laid up and unable to accomplish many of the daily tasks of living, he never complained and was always concerned for my well-being. He was faithful in prayer and continued to obey the Lord in all things. I am forever thankful for his devotion to me and our family.

I am deeply indebted to my family, my son, my daughter and her husband, our friends, and those in the Body of Christ who prayed for my healing.

I extend my love and gratefulness to my spiritual sisters and friends, Minnie Stadler and Kayoung Kim (Pastor Anna) from South Korea, for their empathy and strong devotion to ministering God's healing power.

I am grateful to those who were faithful to bring prophetic words from the Lord that set me free from seeking endorsements for this book.

For all readers, I pray Christ, through your faith, will settle down, abide, and make His permanent home in your hearts. May you be deeply rooted and found secure in His love. May you have the power and strength to apprehend and grasp with all the saints what is the breadth, length, height and depth of His love and realize the blessings of my testimony are available to every believer in Christ. Lastly, dear readers, may you be the recipient of the Divine and respond to the opportunity to live a supernatural lifestyle.

# Introduction

**Come and see what God has done, what**
**awesome miracles He performs for people!**
—Psalm 66:5, NLT

I was having lunch with a friend in a local food
court when a stranger greeted us and started con-
versing with us. To my amazement, he stared into
my eyes and said, "God wants to know, 'Where is
the book?' "

He then focused on my friend and began to
expound on God's desire for her to be filled with
the Holy Spirit. What he did not know is that
we had been talking on this subject just twenty
minutes prior, and he was repeating our conversation. He also did not know God was using
him as a third confirmation that I was to write
this book.

My deepest desire is to impart revelation to the Body of Christ from my personal experience of a holy visitation and almost four decades of studying God's Word at the feet of Jesus Christ.

I sense our heavenly Father's heart for His children to be mature in Christ and empowered to do the "greater works" of Christ. I sense the great desire and steadfast perseverance of God through the Holy Spirit to equip us in these last days to magnify the Lord and bring Him glory; for it is written:

*Truly, truly, I say to you, whoever believes in me will also do the works that I do; and greater works than these will he do, because I am going to the Father. Whatever you ask in my name, this I will do, that the Father may be glorified in the Son. If you ask me anything in my name, I will do it.*

—John 14:12-14

Developing an intimate relationship with Jesus Christ is the foundation to entering a supernatural relationship with the Father, Son, and Holy Spirit. God wants your relationship with Him to be abundantly alive with love and wholeness in body, soul, and spirit. Jesus wants to be your friend. Best friends love one another and share everything. It is written, *"It is your Father's good pleasure to give you the kingdom"* (Luke 12:32). His Kingdom is full of love, power, authority and a great inheritance of treasures accessible to mature believers who seek to be FULL of Christ.

In these pages you will find practical advice to *"press on toward the goal for the prize of the upward call of God in Christ Jesus"* (Philippians 3:14) through pure pursuit of a deeper, loving relationship with Him.

*~Lucille Parkerson*

PART 1

# Embracing the King

# First Light

Remember the things I have done in the past,
For I alone am God!
I am God, and there is none like me.
Only I can tell you the future
before it even happens.
Everything I plan will come to pass,
for I do  whatever I wish.
—Isaiah 46:9-10, NLT

THERE IS A DEAD-END STREET IN CLINTON, Maryland, with small houses—just a handful— close enough to each other that the children can be heard playing outside at either end of the street. Our yard was larger than most and backed up to a cluster of trees. We couldn't see it from our house, but just beyond the trees was a small white Baptist church on another road. In that little church, I heard the message of Christ's salvation and believed it, and this was the beginning of my Christian life.

In my earliest remembrance of Jesus being in my life, I had a sense that He was watching over me. The small rural church was partitioned into sections, with drapery surrounding humble wooden benches. We would sing hymns, pray, and hear stories of Jesus and all that He accomplished for us. Church, to me, was a happy place, a place I desired to be and a wonderful respite from the turmoil in our home.

On one particular Sunday after church, as little girls will do, I merrily skipped and leaped through our backyard to the house. I was so filled with the message of hope and faith that it made me happy. As I entered our house, I approached my father, delighted to share what I had learned in Sunday school.

He was sitting in a chair drinking beer, and I blurted out how much he needed Jesus in his life, a message that was music to my ears but definitely not to his. He lashed out at me with a loud voice saying there was no God and "when you die, you die." In my childhood innocence, I was not prepared for this harsh response or such conflict. His words stung me and made me feel very small and very sad. I walked away and thought about what I knew to be true and thought about his response, and I knew in my heart that he was wrong.

My mother was raised in a large Catholic family in beautiful Puerto Rico. She first sought out a connection with the Catholic Church when she moved to the mainland of the United States, but decided on attending an Episcopal church located a few miles from our home. On Sundays, my father would drop us off at church and then head a short distance to a local bar to pass the time. Later, when church was over, he picked us up and drove us home. We lived unaware of the dangers of riding in a car with a drunk driver. Even back then we must have had heavenly intervention.

When Dad was in no condition to drive us to church, we walked. We were four little girls conditioned by circumstances beyond our control. Our lives reflected the dead-end street we lived on. What hope was there for children born into a family in turmoil from alcohol and unbelief?

For me, just about any day I was not at home was a good day. Mom was my saving grace, for she was loving, kind, and nurturing, and I loved and admired her deeply. Despite our hardships, she never complained and never spoke badly of our father. She would always say, "Your father is a good provider," and that was the end of the conversation.

Besides Sunday school, I delighted in an occasional summer Vacation Bible School. One particular summer was different because the lessons were on how Jesus wanted us to be baptized in water and the meaning of that baptism. Oh, I so wanted to be baptized! I begged Mom to have me baptized. All the necessary arrangements were made with the priest, and I was baptized when I was ten.

From the time I learned about Jesus, I talked to Him every day. One night, before I fell asleep, I made a bold request to Heaven: "Bless me with a loving spouse, a son, a daughter, and a home." I then promised to do whatever He wanted me to do. Believe me, God hears the prayers of a child.

We moved to a larger house just as I was entering junior high school and, consequently, we were no longer in walking distance of a church. During these years we experienced a steady decline in family relationships. Dad drank more heavily and suffered a debilitating stroke, which left him paralyzed on one side of his body. He could no longer work, his driving was limited, and so he was now homebound. For all of these reasons (and perhaps others that I cannot explain), we simply stopped attending church, and all positive influences on our lives seemed to dry up.

On two occasions, Mom took us and left, when the shadow of greater darkness became evident. Once, when we were young, we temporarily relocated to Puerto Rico. When we were in our teens, we temporarily relocated to Florida. Mom was drawn to both of these locations to be nearer to family members.

These flights and relocations were very difficult for us. Life was hard, especially for Mom, who was trying to keep food on the table and make ends meet. In those days, assistance, or social programs, did not exist to help women and children in dire circumstances. Then, as suddenly as we had arrived at a new location, we would be returned home, as our father would come looking to retrieve us. Mother always forgave him, and the cycle would begin all over again.

Then one day God placed a Christian man in my path. In retrospect, I realize that he was a sidewalk evangelist. He talked to me about Jesus and handed me a little red pocket Bible. It described our need for God and His solution for bringing us to Him. In that small booklet, there were encouraging Bible verses. Although we had left God, He was still watching over us.

# CHAPTER 2

# Light from Light

WE RETURNED TO MARYLAND, AND I had begun attending a new high school when I experienced my first miracle. Before boarding the school bus to return home one day, a friend ran up to me and begged me to come home with her. I had a check in my spirit—Mom wouldn't approve—but I yielded to my friend's strong influence.

Her plan was to travel with an older classmate in his car. I called home and left a message with Dad of my intentions and told him, "Just tell Mom I'm going to Harriet's." There were six of us in the car, three in the front and three in the back. I sat behind the driver. The only person I knew in the group was my friend, and she was sitting next to me.

Not far from the school, we crossed a busy intersection. As we were crossing over, I turned to my left and saw a car careening at full speed down a hill straight toward my door. I screamed out to God and flung myself across the laps of the other two occupants beside me. After that, I don't remember anything.

I thought I had died and gone to Heaven. I was surrounded by shining, bright lights, and everything was white. Then I began to hear muffled voices and realized I was face down on a white sheet in a hospital operating room. The doctors were suturing a nasty wound on the back of my head. I spent a week in the hospital under a doctor's care for a concussion.

When I returned to school, my friends began to fill me in on the rumors of the crash. They said I had been picked up by an ambulance and had been dead on arrival. I later discovered the truth: that a volunteer firefighter driving a school bus had pulled over at the accident scene to offer assistance and had found me unconscious. He performed mouth-to-mouth resuscitation to revive me. God used this man to bring me back to life. Some months later, I presented my rescuer with a life-saving award at a banquet for heroes.

Following this harrowing event, I realized God had turned it all for my good (see Genesis 50:20), for now my whole life changed for the better. A financial settlement provided a car, giving me the ability to work part time. I began working long hours and weekends at sixteen and was now able to buy my own clothes, pay my own bills, and give my parents money for my car insurance. I felt propelled and empowered to do well in school so I could achieve my dreams of graduation, federal employment, falling in love, getting married, and having children. Having been a witness to my mother's difficult life, I was very independent; I never wanted to be dependent on anyone.

Not long after this I met Richard Parkerson, who became my high school sweetheart and, later, my husband. I may have been young, but I knew how to pray with purpose and promise, and I had believed God would grant me a divine love connection, intersecting and weaving my path with the one He would choose for me. I fell crazy in love with this guy. He was kind, caring, and responsible and seemed much more mature than anyone I knew. After several years of dating, we married.

We both continued working and pursuing higher education, and we also had two beautiful children. All my prayers had been answered exactly as I had requested. It was a time of new beginnings, building a family and also a fresh, new life with the living God.

Raising and nurturing our children gave me an even deeper appreciation for the Giver of Life. I found wonder and awe in His creation, in the mystery of childbearing and rearing, and in the enormous responsibility of it all. I pondered the future and how my children would turn out. I thought I had turned out well, in spite of my difficult upbringing and circumstances, and, with God's help, I was determined that my children would too.

I was always thirsty for more of Jesus. This little light of mine desired more light from Him. One day I was listening to my favorite rock-and-roll station on the car radio, and twice the tuner jumped to a Christian station. I fidgeted the tuner several times, attempting to find my station, and when the light finally came on again, it was clear that God was trying to talk to me, and He was doing it through Christian radio. I decided to listen, and I liked what I heard so much that this station became my new favorite.

Over time, I grew in knowledge and faith and was determined to learn as much as I could about my heavenly Father. I found a historical Episcopal church nearby, and we made it our home church. It was there that I learned the Bible by teaching a preschool class, which my children attended. We were all growing spiritually. Personally, I was devouring the Bible and gaining understanding.

Then I heard about the Holy Spirit for the first time and was born from above (see John 3:7). The result was that my zeal for the Lord increased ... until it was recognized by church leadership. The rector recommended that I meet with him weekly, as he earnestly desired me to consider working toward ordination to the ministry. This was all quite surprising. I had thought that everyone probably had a similar journey or spiritual trajectory. Nevertheless, I agreed to meet with him.

Our meetings were spiritually enriching, and I looked forward to them, but I knew God had not called me to be an Episcopal priest. The meetings ended when I declined candidacy, and the rector returned, with renewed zeal, to the mission field.

It was during our young adult years that Rich also made a profession of faith, and he, too, was born from above and filled with the Holy Spirit. We received spiritual gifts and impartations in a small Charismatic church, where the Holy Spirit was honored and anticipated at every meeting. His Spirit was also at work in our simple, everyday lives. Light was also received from a Christ-centered community where our children attended Christian school.

Rich and I were now biblical believers, committed to the Lord and the Body of Christ. Our life was good in every way, and that lasted for a very long time. We were truly blessed. We were all thriving—spiritually, physically, relationally, and financially. In time, our children went on to college and started pursuing their own dreams.

Our daughter met the love of her life, a pastor's son, and married him. We were ecstatic, over the moon with joy, working hard toward our career goals and planning for our retirements.

# CHAPTER 3

# Light for My Path

---

JUST ONE YEAR LATER, EVERYTHING changed. I was stopped at a local traffic light one day while driving home from work and was, suddenly and without warning, violently jolted. My car had been rear-ended by a truck. The driver had come off of a major highway and had swerved into a left-turn lane and then couldn't stop. My car was trust forward, the rear end came off the ground, and my body was violently shaken.

In a daze, I thought, "What just happened?"

The driver of the truck was very apologetic and said his foot had become stuck between the brake and gas pedal. But that didn't help things. I was seriously shaken up.

But as I examined myself, I didn't seem to have any serious injuries, so I went on home. Later that night I had the worst neck pain I had ever experienced. My entire spine seemed to be in electrical shock, with sparklers firing nonstop into all my extremities.

Gradually my entire muscle system began to harden, and I had knotted muscles, muscle spasms, and a tingling, burning sensation throughout the entire body. I could hear my heart beating in my ears. With every heartbeat, my whole body was throbbing. In desperation, I cried and cried and cried some more, and kept repeating, "Somebody DO something!" If you can imagine hitting your thumb with a hammer, you know how that will throb. But imagine your whole body throbbing in that way, all at once.

I was diagnosed with a class IV spinal cord injury to the neck, post-traumatic fibromyalgia, pulsatile tinnitus, and myofascial pain syndrome. The doctor told me I would always live with pain and said I should stop working. I was advised to apply for permanent disability and seek pain management advice. But I refused to throw in the towel.

For ten months I struggled to hold on to my job, by working part time and alternating working between home and office. But even that proved too much for me. As much as I did not want to accept defeat, it seemed impossible to keep working. Pain levels would increase with activity, and every couple of hours I needed to lie down and recuperate.

My only relief from chronic pain was to knock myself out with sleeping pills or rest intermittently, Afterwards it was difficult to resume activity.

I went to many doctors for any form of improvement—surgeons, internists, neurologists, massage therapists, an acupuncturist, and chiropractors (including an orthogonal chiropractor). I prayed daily for healing and tried to keep a positive attitude. With each new doctor or alternative remedy, I experienced hope followed by disappointment.

After three to five weeks of bed rest,  my muscles began to lose strength and tone. We thought if we could massage the muscles in spasm perhaps this would increase blood circulation and promote healing. The massages proved to be very painful and did not provide much relief.

I regularly went to a pain management doctor for years. He treated me with scads of prescriptions and various remedies, but there was no lasting relief.

As the pain continued throughout my body, I developed an overwhelming feeling of the need for "flight." I was constantly thinking of ways to find comfort and peace and went from pillar to post, thinking that something or someone would figure this thing out and bring me wholeness. The side effects of some of my medications decreased my quality of life, making me dizzy, sleepy, woozy, and just feeling "out of it." Sleep aids remained my only comfort.

One night, in the middle of the night, I heard a suggestion: "Why don't you just kiss your husband goodbye, get your car keys, and drive away, and when you see a wall, run into it?" Half asleep and half awake, I remember answering the sinister suggestion by saying that my life was not my own. I had no authority to end it because my life belonged to Jesus Christ.

We continued praying for healing and experienced some lessening of the intensity of the nerve storm in my body, but major obstacles remained. Not all neck and back pain was eliminated. I was thankful to be able to take a shower without feeling like the drops of water were shards of glass. I often explained to those who would ask about my condition, "Have you ever hit your elbow and felt a surge of tingling and burning going down the arm and into the hand?" The difference was that my symptoms never left me and they affected my whole body—nonstop, twenty-four hours a day and seven days a week.

This went on for years. I felt terrible every day, even though I did not look disabled. I could still walk, talk, and dress myself, but my physical activity was limited by the pain that would spike and ebb. My eyes were glassy all the time, and people told me they could see the pain in my eyes. Physicians could hear my heart beating up in my face.

Month after month and year after year, doctors would palpate muscles to confirm spasms and inject them with lidocaine. Plus I used pain patches, spinal blocks and sleeping pills, and still it was not enough.

Despite all of this,  the prominent insurance company handling our claim failed to be a good neighbor, refusing to settle. We fought a court battle and lost. There was absolutely no compensation for medical bills and no punitive damages. In short, there was no justice.

But God had not forsaken us. He provided for us and, by His grace, we forgave and prayed for the offender's salvation and blessings. My hope was in God all day long every day, and I envisioned that I would one day be restored.

Every day I cried out to Jesus, my Healer. My constant prayers were mirrored in the psalms:

*I am suffering and in pain.*
*Rescue me, O God, by your saving power.*

*Then I will praise God's name with singing*
*and I will honor him with thanksgiving.*
*For this will please the LORD...*
                                    —Psalm 69:29-31, NLT

Every visit to the pain management doctor re-
quired a full written description of all symptoms
and a determination of the pain level I was suffering, and this caused me to constantly repeat the
negatives. Without realizing it, I was giving away
my power and allowing greater darkness to inhabit my body. I had a lot to learn about healing.

PART II

# Kingdoms
# and Manifestations

# CHAPTER 4

# Light That Reveals Darkness

**Whoever believes in me
may not remain in darkness.**
—John 12:46

THE WISE CHRISTIAN RECOGNIZES spiritual warfare emanating from the kingdom of darkness and counteracts it with an arsenal from the Kingdom of Light. Jesus taught us to pray, *"Deliver us from evil"* (Matthew 6:13).

Christians cannot be totally taken over by darkness, but the enemy can attack anywhere we give him a foothold. In other words, we must resist the fallen one, and when we do, he will flee (see James 4:7). If we do not resist him, we are condoning his actions, and he will have a legal and spiritual right to continue to operate in or upon us. The apostle Paul wrote:

*Let us cleanse ourselves from all filthiness of the flesh and spirit, perfecting holiness.*
—2 Corinthians 7:1, KJV

## UNDERSTANDING UNCLEAN SPIRITS

Any area that is not under the Holy Spirit's control gives free reign to an unclean spirit. The mission of an unclean spirit is to stop one from being a Christian and to steal, kill, and destroy. If you tolerate an unclean spirit, it will stay and continue to torment you. For the unbeliever, the torment will be eternal. The believer receives eternal salvation but forfeits the abundant life Jesus came to give us (see John 10:10.)

The Greek word translated here as *abundant* is *perisson*, meaning "to the full, till it overflows; a greater life, an exceeding life, a life of advantage, or preeminence." A life of sickness, pain, and disease is not the abundant life; it is spiritual warfare and it started in the Garden of Eden. Sickness and disease came into the world through Adam's disobedience.

Guess who beguiled Adam to sin? It was the fallen one, the prince of the kingdom of darkness. Please believe me, Christian, anything that is not from Heaven is from the flesh or from the kingdom of darkness.

I believe and know that God living in us can overcome anything, and that includes unclean spirits. Such spirits feed upon wounds. Such a wound might be physical, spiritual, or emotional. We must yield our body, soul, and spirit to God's righteousness and be holy.

A wound of this type can begin with a backache, a leg ache, or a headache, a relationship breakup, a grievance, or any type of trauma. If we do not resist it, we may be condoning the darkness that is attempting to inhabit us.

But we are made in God's image, and there is no record of Jesus having any of these things. Jesus was completely human and completely divine at the same time. We were also created to be completely human and completely divine.

Another important area of spiritual warfare concerns how spirits affect the animal kingdom or the natural realm. The presence and depth of spiritual light or darkness affects the animal kingdom, the earth, and the land. When there is violence and bloodshed (spiritual darkness), the land mourns, and all living things begin to languish, to the point of death (see Genesis 8:1, Job 38:41, Hosea 4:3 and Romans 8:19-22).

## LESSONS LEARNED

In the years before and after the car accident that changed my life, I experienced some unusual events. At the time, I was unaware of their spiritual significance. There were signs that I should have recognized as spiritual warfare. I share these events with you as "lessons learned":

1. One lovely morning I went into our kitchen and found that a very aggressive mouse had been gnawing at the base of our kitchen door, attempting to gain access to the kitchen through the laundry room. We cleaned up the mess and set a mouse trap, but we didn't catch it. We decided to declare God's Word over the house and ask Him to keep pests out, and we had no further problems.

2. As I was watching TV in our family room one day, a large bat suddenly appeared. It flew past me at eye level and went through the entrance of the hallway toward the bedrooms. We turned on lights behind it and turned off lights where it was headed, and then we trapped it. Opening a large window, we pushed it out, using a six-foot win-

dow screen as a shield. Thinking back on it, we had no idea how the bat had gained entry to the house. In those days, however, I remembered speaking worldly expressions like, "The car came out of nowhere, like a bat out of Hell." Was that coincidence or invitation? The Scriptures teach: *"For out of the abundance of the heart the mouth speaks. A good person out of his good treasure of the heart brings forth good"* (Matthew 12:34-35).

3. One evening I was walking from the family room to the hallway leading to our bedroom. There are two steps down to the hallway, so I turned on the light to navigate those steps and saw a snake lying there on the rug. Hearing my loud shriek, my husband came and removed it.

4. One evening in a home Bible study, we had just finished a meal with a small group of friends and Rich was beginning to teach when I was physically attacked by the host's black cat. I had been seated at the dining room table, and had done nothing to provoke the cat. Suddenly it jumped on my back and, in the process of sliding down to the floor, clawed my arms.

5. One day I wanted to investigate some strange noises that seemed to come from the roof in the front of our house. I grabbed a coat, walked into the front yard and looked up, and there I discovered a large flock of buzzards sitting on our roof. I was able to chase them away with clapping and shouting.

6. Several times, when Rich and I were in bed asleep, I heard voices of laughter and communication and was awakened by them. This was so strange that I began to wonder if I had been dreaming or was experiencing discernment of spiritual activity.

It is a given that fatigue and lack of energy are byproducts of suffering pain, but they can also indicate spiritual oppression. Darkness steals energy, just as light produces energy. The culmination of all of these signs signaled spiritual warfare and led me to seek healing and deliverance. I had to get over my spiritual pride and no longer care what anyone called it. I just wanted it GONE! After years of suffering pain, although I had been doing all the right things, I felt like a dim light. Now I began to change some things.

For one, I began to change the way I read the Bible. By changing the sentence structure, I turned each scripture into a prayer request and used it to cry out to Jesus to fill me with more of His light and help me to overcome the enemy.

*A dimly burning wick He will not quench.*
                              Isaiah 42:3, AMPC

I remember praying this scripture like this: *"Lord God, You said I could ask for more of Your light!"* This is His promise that, even though our light is feeble or dim, Jesus, the Messiah, will take care not to quench even a small flame of devotion to Him. Instead, He will tend it, trimming the wick and adding fresh oil, so that it may burn more brightly for His glory.

My church did not teach on the promises of God, on healing or miracles, on the gifts of the Holy Spirit or how we operate in those gifts, or how to live a supernatural lifestyle. There I heard no teachings on who we are in Christ when we are born from above or on the authority Jesus has given His followers. But, thank God, there are many Christian books and TV programs on these subjects. Thank God for all those who have testified of His glorious deeds. Thank God for all those in Christ who live a supernatural lifestyle and are willing to share their faith, scriptures, and experiences.

God's children do not have to grovel for His mercy. In every challenge, we are to declare His Word and promises and confess who we are and what Christ has given us. I was declaring healing by boldly confessing the scriptures every day, and then I was waiting patiently for healing to manifest.

For those of you who are reading this book, I trust you are already searching for His promise for your given situation. Once you have found it, begin to speak it out and keep doing that until you receive your breakthrough.

There are approximately seven thousand scriptures relating to the promises of God. Ask Him to enlighten your understanding through them. According to Psalm 91, God's promises are our armor and protection. Do you have your armor on?

God's Word is alive (see Hebrews 4:12). His words are LIFE, and they are health and healing to our flesh (see Proverbs 4:22). Our faith will grow by *"hearing"* His Word (Romans 10:17). I personalized His Word and read it out loud so that my ears could hear it. It entered my heart, my soul, and my spirit and began to work in my body.

*I attend to God's Word.*
*I incline my ears to His sayings.*
*I will not let them depart from my eyes.*
*I will keep (or hide) God's words in the midst of*
*my heart.*
*God's Word is LIFE to me.*
*I have found God's words to be HEALTH to ALL*
*MY FLESH.*
          —Proverbs 4:20-22, author's paraphrase

You can take His Word every day as medicine to heal the flesh, for it is clear from all the promises of good health in His Word that the Father wants His children to be physically well.

One evening, as I was worshiping, a familiar verse of scripture raced across my mind, and I began to claim it just for me:

*All of you together are Christ's body, and each of*
*you is a part of it … . God has appointed for the*
*church: first are apostles, second are prophets,*
*third are teachers, then those who do miracles,*
***those who have the gift of healing.***
          —1 Corinthians 12:27-28, NLT
          (emphasis added)

In that moment, I raised my voice and prayed, "Lord, send me the person in the Body of Christ who has the gift of healing." Things always began to happen when I prayed His Word. For one thing, faith rose up in me. I told God that I believed all His Word and knew He could and would send me help. We have Heaven's attention when we start declaring we believe ALL His Word.

I heard a woman Bible teacher say that most people don't realize their angels are sitting around bored, not doing anything. She said the angels can only do what God says in His Word (see Psalm 103:20). By speaking His Word, we can release our angels to go forth to work with us, and they won't be bored anymore. In everything they do, they will bring glory to God.

It is important to note that the Father has already given us everything we need to live an abundant and victorious life here and now. He gave His only Son, Jesus Christ, as the Passover Lamb who took away the sins of the world (see John 1:29). When we accept what Jesus Christ did for us and publicly confess that He is Lord, the Father brings us into His family. Then the righteousness of Christ transfers from Heaven to cover us, and we become the children of God (see 2 Corinthians 5:21).

This adoption by the Father is just the beginning of us transforming from a natural or human being to a supernatural being. He then calls us to subdue the earth, for He has put us in charge of His Creation. God has said:

> *Be fruitful and multiply and fill the earth and subdue it, and have dominion.*
>
> —Genesis 1:28

In our natural world, there is order and a chain of command. Unless you are self-employed, you have a boss. He or she gives assignments and instructions about fulfilling those assignments and has an expectation of an outcome. If a problem arises, you may go back and ask for additional wisdom or direction, but it is still up to you to complete the assignment. Right?

The natural world was created by God and is a reflection of His supernatural domain. God told us that He has given us everything we need to live on the earth and prosper. Then He forgave us for all sin through His Son.

Remember, when Christ died He said, *"It is finished"* (John 19:30). Christ did everything He was called to do:

- He took the penalty for our sins and forgave us our sins.

- Through the stripes He bore for us, He took upon Himself all of our diseases and sicknesses (see Isaiah 53).
- He instructed us to be born from above and to seek and receive the promised Holy Spirit.
- And He provided a new supernatural and abundant life for us. That is His plan for every person He created.

Christ Jesus triumphed over all His enemies (see Colossians 2:15). Then He gave to His followers everything the Father had given Him. So, it is time for us to mature in Christ.

This is where the Church, the Body of Christ, has fallen short. Many have not understood who they are, as children of God, and have not matured to the full stature of Christ. It is written, *"In Christ [we] are all sons [and daughters] of God"* (Galatians 3:26). Peter wrote:

*You are a chosen race, a royal priesthood, a holy nation, a people for his own possession, that you may proclaim the excellencies of him who called you out of darkness into his marvelous light.*
—1 Peter 2:9

Believer, the Kingdom of God lives within us, and we are already *"seated in heavenly places,"* even as our Lord prepares a table and a home for us in Heaven. When a group of very religious people asked Jesus when the Kingdom of God would come, He answered them:

> *For behold, the kingdom of God is within you [in your hearts] and among you [surrounding you].*
>                       —Luke 17:21, AMPC

### God's Answer

I continued proclaiming God's Word: *"Lord, send me the person in the Body of Christ who has the gift of healing."* One afternoon Rich came home, after having coffee and donuts at a local shop called the Donut Connection, and began to tell me about the lady who had waited on him. She was Korean, and I immediately thought of our unmarried son who had visited Korea and found Asian women very attractive. I began to ask Rich about this woman. Was she attractive? Was she married? He wasn't sure, so we decided to visit the shop together that coming weekend.

That evening all hope of sleep escaped me, and I kept hearing, "You need to see the Korean woman in the morning." The next morning I shared my evening of restless sleep with Rich and how, in the process, I had been instructed to go to the donut shop right away. So I went.

The donut shop was busy that day, and this was very frustrating for me. There were so many customers. How was I ever going to be able to speak to the woman behind the counter? I silently prayed for an opportunity to open up a conversation.

In the meantime, I lost my perspective of connecting her to my son and wasn't sure why I had been led there or how to get started. Finally, the line of customers dwindled and no one else appeared.

I began the conversation by admiring the cross the lady wore around her neck, and the moment I mentioned Jesus, she blossomed. We had a lovely conversation that day.

Her name was Minnie, and something was said that led to her talking about healing. I told her of my own need for a touch from God, and with great compassion, she listened. As she did, she actually began weeping. We exchanged information, and she invited me to her home for a visit. She also wanted me to talk by phone with her pastor, a lady named Anna.

Pastor Anna had a healing and deliverance ministry in Korea, but each year she came to Minnie's home for special meetings. She also prayed for people over the phone and they were healed. When I heard that, faith and expectation flooded my soul.

The opportunity came for me to connect with Pastor Anna, and she prayed fervently over the phone. I didn't understand a word she said, but while she prayed, I suddenly had a vision of being on a seashore. There were sticks in the sand. Those sticks were being pulled out, and the holes were filling up with sand. I knew instantly that healing had just entered my body.

I remembered the story of a woman Jesus had healed. She had touched the hem of His garment, and immediately she could feel in her body that she was healed (see Mark 5:29). I now felt the same. Praise be to God for His indescribable gifts!

Later, Pastor Anna came to America, and I was invited to a healing meeting where she would lay hands on the sick, and they would recover (see Mark 16:18). The Holy Spirit spoke to me and said, "Go, and do whatever Anna says." I was ecstatic with anticipation.

# CHAPTER 5

# Healing Light

---

I READ THE NOTE ON THE EXTERIOR door of the house that said to enter quietly. I gently knocked and tried the door knob. It was unlocked. As I entered, I could hear what sounded like Korean singing, but I recognized the melodies as familiar hymns. The house was filled with people seeking healing, and I could feel the presence of a sweet Spirit.

Pastor Anna spoke very little English. She was praying, anointing the sick with oil, and laying hands on them while we listened to Christian worship music. Each person was asked to lie on a floor mat. We were covered with blankets and/or towels, and she then prayed softly for each one, laying hands on us. This went on for hours.

On three separate occasions, I joined others who were being prayed for by Pastor Anna. On the first occasion, I prayed that the Lord would show me if Anna was being led by His Spirit by having her come and lay hands on a particular area of my body. I did this several times, and every time I made the request, she would respond immediately and precisely to the part of my body that I had asked for healing. In this way, the Lord gave me wonderful confirmations that she was operating under the authority and anointing of the Holy Spirit. While I was in these "healing rooms," I also experienced supernatural visions.

As Pastor Anna placed her hands on us and prayed, we were worshiping the One who sits on Heaven's throne. I had brought along a favorite CD that included a song entitled "Anoint Me." I sang it in my spirit, believing that God would hear my call to anoint me with a greater measure of His Holy Spirit and bring healing and refreshment to my body and soul. During the service the CD player was repeating the lyrics, "anoint me, anoint me, anoint me," and then the anointing came forth.

When it happened, my eyes were closed in prayer and worship. Then, suddenly, beautiful, spiraling lights appeared out of nowhere. They changed to a bright blue light, and that formed into a large spiraling sapphire jewel. All of the magnificent colors I was seeing appeared to be living, constantly changing, charged with brilliance and forming into the large spiraling gem. That precious gem was glowing, and it appeared to be breathing light, a living, creative masterpiece, more brilliant than anything I had ever seen.

Everything God created has meaning—even names, colors, and objects. When the prophet Ezekiel tried to describe a vision he had, he said that the throne of God had appeared as a sapphire:

*There was the likeness of a throne, in appearance like sapphire.*

—Ezekiel 1:26

I discovered that blue is symbolic of healing, and the eternal presence of YAHWEH, the God of Israel, the Creator of all things. This reminds us of His heavenly realm, prayer, priesthood, and authority. It reveals God's grace, His divinity, His Holy Spirit, His overcoming power, and His revelation knowledge. Blue is also symbolic of the truth, the Word of God, the Word that was made flesh, the Messiah, Jesus Christ.

I recognized the brilliant sapphire's color as being the same hue depicted on the flag of the nation of Israel. It has represented the color of

God's chosen people dating back to the time of King David. [1]

I wonder if God's favorite colors are not blue and white. Blue elements cover so much of the earth, from the sky to the pools of water and the world's vast oceans.

Visions of a blue spiraling light continued with each visit to the healing rooms. Then a beautiful green light began to take the shape of a precious gemstone. It formed into a large emerald. It increased in size and became surrounded by blazing orange. The colors were alive—moving, glistening, and changing in depth and breadth.

In Revelation John saw a vision of the throne of God in all its glory and described it as gemstones with the glow of an emerald circling the throne, like a rainbow. [2] Green is symbolic of praise, eternal life, vigor, prosperity, mercy, restoration, health, healing, new beginnings, and freshness. It is said to be symbolic of God's holy seed, harvest, sowing and reaping, immortality, fresh oil, new life, and joy in hope. Scriptural references for this are to be found in Romans 12:12, Psalm 23:2 and 92:14, Genesis 1:30, Luke 23:31 and Revelation 22:2.

---

1. The flag of Israel is blue and white.
2. See Revelation 4:3.

Orange is also symbolic of praise, but also of warfare, passion, power, fire, fruitfulness, joy, and the harvest season.

The presence of the gems reminded me of the jewels worn by the High Priest in the Jewish Temple. He wore an ephod (like an apron or pouch) on his chest (see Exodus 25:7 and Exodus 28). The pouch was about a nine-inch square made of gold, blue, purple, scarlet, and fine linen and embedded with twelve precious stones in rows of four, representing the twelve tribes of Israel. The ephod was worn over the heart of the priest as he entered, to approach God in the Holy of Holies, an inner sanctuary of the Temple.

We, too, as Gentile believers in the God of Israel, were taught through Saint Paul that all believers in Christ have been grafted into a cultivated olive tree. The olive tree represents the chosen nation of Israel, the Jews (see Romans 11:24). Likewise, it is written in Ephesians 3:6 (AMPC):

*Gentiles are now to be fellow heirs [with the Jews], members of the same body and joint partakers [sharing] in the same divine promise in Christ.*

God views us as precious living jewels and gems, just as He views His Jewish children as gems. We are called *living stones* in 1 Peter 2:5 (AMPC):

> *[Come] and, like living stones, be yourselves built [into] a spiritual house...to offer up [those] spiritual sacrifices [that are] acceptable and pleasing to God through Jesus Christ.*

In a study of gemology, I found that there are seven precious stones: amethyst, diamond, emerald, pearl, ruby, opal, and sapphire. All other stones are considered semi-precious. Gem stones are judged by their color, cut, clarity, size, and the amount of water in them. The water is what gives them their luster and their brilliance. To reach their potential, gems must be cut, shaped, cleaned, and polished, and no two stones are alike.

Various treatments enhance the color of a stone, such as heat and the application of oil. Water, heat, and oil are all reminders of the Holy Spirit. So there is much to learn from our Father's describing us as jewels. I believe the Holy Spirit was revealing to me that I was before the throne of God, and there Christ was interceding for His precious gems, for healing and deliverance. The Father's answer is, "Yes, give My children the good benefits of wholeness!"

Jesus Christ is the door through which all humankind may gain entrance to Heaven. He is the Pearl of Great Price. That is why Heaven's gates are made of pearl (see Matthew 13:46).

I could feel healing flowing through Anna. I have since learned that miracles are immediate or instant, and healing can be instantaneous, but it is often the working of our faith accomplished over time. My healing began with Anna's prayer over the phone. Slowly, knotted muscles began to relax in my neck and upper back, and my pain greatly receded.

Anna continued to pray for me for a whole year after imparting healing to my body, and my physical strength kept increasing. At the same times, my spiritual devotion also increased.

Spiritual life is so vividly portrayed in the book of psalms. These psalms record history, prophecy, intercession, communication with God, praise and worship, and so much more. Studying the psalms in depth led me to the personal decision to separate times of intercessory praying and times of worship. In order to increase my intimacy with the Father, Son, and Holy Spirit, I decided to devote time exclusively to worship Him every day without asking Him for anything at all.

His Word declares:

*Delight yourself in the LORD, and he will give
you the desires of your heart.*

—Psalm 37:4

## KNOWING HIM

Relationships are about connecting with and enjoying each another, and our relationship with God should not be any different. From the beginning of time God's utmost desire has been an intimate relationship with His creation— with us.

Jesus said, *"Not everyone who says to me, 'Lord, Lord,' will enter the kingdom of heaven, but the one who does the will of my Father who is in heaven"* (Matthew 7:21). He went on to say that many will speak of all the *"things"* they did for Him (verse 22), and He will answer *"I never KNEW you"* (verse 23, emphasis added).

This word *knew,* translated from the Greek in the New Testament, has the same root meaning as the Hebrew word translated in the Old Testament where it says, *"Adam KNEW Eve"* (Genesis 4:1, emphasis added). There are those who call themselves believers in Jesus, but they have no real intimacy with Him.

Think about the intimate relationship in a marriage. The two become one (see Genesis 2:24 and Mark 10:8). Adam *knew* Eve, meaning that the two of them became one.

**Is Jesus Christ IN you?**

**Are you IN Him?**

**Are you IN the Body of Christ?**

The Body of Christ is composed of many people from many nations who have received Jesus Christ as their Savior and Lord and have completely surrendered to Him. If you are not sure if you are in Christ, there is a prayer for you at the end of this book. If you have surrendered yourself to Jesus Christ and made Him Master of your life, then you can call upon Him in faith and confidence that He will accomplish His Word, because everything you have belongs to Him, and everything He has belongs to you.

One day I was reading a familiar scripture in Malachi 4:2 and discovered another promise from God. He says that if we revere His name He will send the Sun of Righteousness upon us *"with healing in His wings"* (AMPC). This made me think about how I could "revere" His name, and I began asking the Lord how to claim this promise. I desired the Sun of Righteousness to visit me and bring more healing.

I remembered the story of God's true name being hidden from the world by devout Jews in ages past. They knew His exact name in Hebrew but would never publicly disclose it for fear of breaking the commandment not to take His name in vain (see Exodus 20:7). The closest translation of His name in English is YAHWEH. In the hallelu *"jah"* (*jah* or *Yah*), we are actually praising God's name.

Yes, dear Christian, call upon His name. Call upon His name, as we are instructed in Malachi 4:2. Adore Him, and adore His name! His Word is TRUTH, and His Word will never return void (see Isaiah 55:11). Now the gates of Heaven opened up to me, as I called upon my precious Redeemer, Jesus Christ, Beloved of God the Father, and He came with healing in His wings.

Every evening, I sang a new song to the Lord, honoring, admiring, and revering His name, His titles, His character, calling out and singing each identifier individually. "I will declare that Your name stands firm forever. I will declare that Your righteousness is established in the heavens. I declare You are my Advocate. I declare You are the Almighty," etc. Ask the Holy Spirit to give you a new song with a new tune, and sing out His marvelous, wonderful names. He is the:

| | |
|---|---|
| Advocate | 1 John 2:1 |
| Almighty | Exodus 6:3 |
| Alpha and Omega | Revelation 1:8 |
| Amen | Revelation 3:14 |
| Ancient of Days | Daniel 7:9 |
| Angel of His Presence | Isaiah 63:9 |
| Anointed Above All Others | Psalm 45:7 |
| Anointed (the Lord's) | Psalm 2:2 |
| Apostle of Our Confession | Hebrews 3:1 |
| Arm of the Lord | Isaiah 51:9 |
| Author and Finisher (Of Our Faith) | Hebrews 12:2 (KJV) |
| Author of Eternal Salvation | Hebrews 5:9 |

I believe that as you meditate upon His name and declare His name, you will begin to feel the power of God rise up in you. He is the:

| | |
|---|---|
| Begotten of God | Hebrews 1:5 |
| Beloved | Matthew 3:17 |
| Blessed | 1 Timothy 6:15 |
| Branch | Zechariah 3:8 |
| Branch of Righteousness | Jeremiah 23:5 & 33:15 |
| Branch (from the root of Jesse) | Isaiah 11:1 & 10 |
| Bread of Life | John 6:35 |
| Bright Morning Star | Revelation 22:16 |

We declare that He is the Captain of the Lord's army in Joshua 5:15, and He is also the:

| | |
|---|---|
| Carpenter's Son | Matthew 13:55 |
| Chief Cornerstone | 1 Peter 2:6 (AMPC) |
| Chief of Ten Thousand | SOS 5:10 (AMPC) |
| Chosen One | Isaiah 42:1 |
| Christ | 530+ times |
| Christ the Lord | Luke 2:11 |
| Christ Jesus our Lord | Romans 8:39 |
| Christ the Power of God | 1 Corinthians 1:24 |
| Counselor | Isaiah 9:6 |
| Covenant for the People | Isaiah 42:6 |
| Dayspring | Luke 1:78 (KJV) |
| Daystar (Morning Star) | 2 Peter 1:19 (KJV) |
| Deliverer | Romans 11:26 |
| Door | John 10:9 |
| Emmanuel | Isaiah 7:14 & 8:8 |
| Eternal Life | 1 John 5:11 |
| Everlasting Father | Isaiah 9:6 |
| Ever Present | Ezekiel 48:35 |

We declare, Lord, that You are Faithful and True (Revelation 19:11), and we declare that You live in us, and You are the:

| | |
|---|---|
| Faithful Witness | Revelation 1:5 |
| Firstbegotten | Hebrews 1:6 (KJV) |
| Firstfruits | 1 Corinthians 15:23 |
| First and Last | Revelation 22:13 |
| Foundation Stone | Isaiah 28:16 |
| Guardian | 1 Peter 2:25 (AMPC) |
| Glorious Lord | Isaiah 33:21 (KJV) |
| God of Israel | Psalm 68:8 |
| God With Us | Matthew 1:23 |
| Great God | Titus 2:13 |
| Great High Priest | Hebrews 4:14 |

Keep pressing into Him! Call upon His name. He promises to bless you.

Christ is the Head of the Body (Colossians 1:18). He is the Head over ALL things, which means He is the Head of Heaven and Earth. He has dominion in the heavens. The angels belong to Him, and He directs them to minister to us. He is reigning on the Earth through us.

We declare He is the:

| | |
|---|---|
| Heir of All Things | Hebrews 1:2 |
| Healer | Exodus 15:26 |
| Holy One of Israel | Isaiah 54:5 |
| Hope of Glory | Colossians 1:27 |

| | |
|---|---|
| I AM | Exodus 3:14-15 & John 8:58 |
| Image of God | Colossians 1:15 |
| Immanuel | Isaiah 7:14 |

By now you should be feeling the Holy Spirit rising up in you. As you mediate upon who Christ is, the fire of God will increase in you, and the Light of Christ will increase in you as well.

We declare that our God is:

| | |
|---|---|
| Jesus Christ our Lord | Romans 1:4 |
| Judge of Israel | Isaiah 30:18 & Micah 5:1 |
| King of Glory | Psalm 24:8-10 |
| King Over All | Zechariah 14:9 |
| Lamb of God | John 1:29 |
| Light of the World | Psalm 27:1 & John 8:12 |
| Lily of the Valleys | Song of Solomon 2:1 |
| Living Bread | John 6:51 |
| Lord God Almighty | Revelation 15:3 (KJV) |
| Lord and Savior | 2 Peter 2:20 |
| Lord of All | Acts 10:36 |
| Lord our Righteousness | Jeremiah 23:6 (AMPC) |
| Lord, your Redeemer | Isaiah 43:14 |
| Love | 1 John 4:8, 16 |

He is the great God of love, for He laid down His life for us. Praise God! Stay the course, and continue revering His name, and you will reap heavenly benefits.

Meditate upon Christ as the Man of Sorrows (Isaiah 53:3). Remember all He did for us when He suffered on the cross and took the penalty for our sins. He triumphs over all powers of darkness as the Master (Matthew 23:10, AMPC), our Majesty (Hebrews 1:3), and the Messiah (Daniel 9:25, KJV).

We declare Him as the:

| | |
|---|---|
| Mighty God | Genesis 17:1 & Isaiah 9:6 |
| Mighty One | Isaiah 60:16 |
| Most Holy | Daniel 9:24 (KJV) |
| Most Mighty | Psalm 45:3 (KJV) |
| Nazarene | Matthew 2:23 |

He is the only wise God (1 Timothy 1:17, KJV), our Passover (1 Corinthians 5:7), and our Great Physician (Exodus 15:26 and Luke 4:23). Let Him speak to you through who He is. Ask Him now to give you further revelation on His character and being.

He is our Provider (Genesis 22:14), our Protector (Psalm 91:2, GNT), and our Righteousness (Jeremiah 23:6).

Our God is the:

| | |
|---|---|
| Prince of Peace | Judges 6:24 & Isaiah 9:6 |
| Prince of the Kings | Revelation 1:5 (KJV) |
| Prophet | Deuteronomy 18:15-18 |
| Propitiation | |
| (Substitution for Our Sins) | Romans 3:25 |
| Rabbi (Teacher) | John 1:49 & John 3:2 |
| Redeemer | Isaiah 59:20 |
| Resurrection | John 11:25 |
| Righteous Servant | Isaiah 53:11 |
| Rock | 1 Corinthians 10:4 |
| Rose of Sharon | Song of Solomon 2:1 |
| Savior of the World | 1 John 4:14 |
| Seed of David | John 7:42 (through Joseph) |
| Seed of a Woman | Genesis 3:15 (through Mary) |
| Shepherd | Psalm 23:1 & John 10:11 |
| Shield | Genesis 15:1 |
| Son of God | Romans 1:4 |
| Son of Man | Acts 7:56 |
| Son of Mary | Mark 6:3 |
| Son of the Highest | Luke 1:32 (KJV) |
| Star (Jacob's) | Numbers 24:17 |
| Sun of Righteousness | Malachi 4:2 |
| Supreme | Psalm 99:2 (GNT) |

The prophet Isaiah declared Christ to be our Sure Foundation (28:16, KJV). The apostle John

(3:2) proclaimed Christ as the Teacher (John 3:2). John further declared Christ as the Truth. Truth is a person, the person of Jesus Christ (John 14:6, AMPC).

Saint Paul spoke of Christ as the Unspeakable Gift given to the world (2 Corinthians 9:15, KJV). Magnify Christ with me.

Declare that He is the:

| | |
|---|---|
| Way | John 14:6 |
| Wonderful | Isaiah 9:6 |
| Word of God | John 1:14 & Revelation 19:13 |

As I continued to declare and revere His name, giving Him honor, praise, and glory, I could feel His presence and sensed that I had received Heaven's attention.

I called upon Him according to Exodus 3:6 and 3:14:

*I am the God of your father, the God of Abraham, the God of Isaac, and the God of Jacob.*
                                        —Exodus 3:6

I declared: "Yes, Lord, You are the God of Abraham, the God of Isaac, and the God of Jacob." I reaffirmed Him as Supreme over me and over my body, soul, and spirit.

Make your praises glorious. Make them loud and make them joyous. Dance before the King of all kings and bring continuous praise to Abba Father, King Jesus, the Son of God. Then watch as the Holy Spirit opens wide the gates of Heaven to you.

## MY HEALING CONTINUED

Early one morning, as I slept lightly, I felt a strange sensation in my lower back. I had a vision of a feather encircling my lumbar spine. Wow! I knew that God would come and fulfill His Word. I could feel a heavenly feather, from the wings of God, sent to provide healing to my lower back.

On another occasion, I awoke from a deep sleep and in my spirit I saw a glimpse of an angel. He was looking down on me from far above my bed. The vision appeared transparent, overlaying the natural ceiling. I could still see, in my mind's eye (like having a thought photo), an unusual looking warrior angel hovering over me. Through a mist, standing behind what looked like a four-foot-high balcony wall, there he was, just looking at me. A large helmet covered his head. It had a slight shield that covered the sides of his face. I could only see the upper half of his body, but it appeared that he was attired with full body armor. He was awesome!

I was comforted by his appearance and had no fear. I felt like he was waiting for just the right moment to strike the enemy. I kept praising God.

*I give thanks to you, O LORD my God, with my whole heart, and I will glorify your name forever.*
                                              —Psalm 86:12

Giving glory to God's name and taking part in faithful, devoted praise resulted in spiritual manifestations of His glory, with signs and wonders. After another evening of praise and worship, I was awakened hearing the words, "You are in the presence of evil." I thought about the warrior angel. Maybe he was issuing this warning. It had not been an audible voice but, rather, an internal voice, one in my head. I have to admit that I was very fearful this time, yet the command was clear. I was instructed: "Tell it to leave."

I arose and woke my husband, and we began to pray together. We declared the greatness of God and that we belonged to Him. Then we told the unclean spirit, or demon of darkness, to leave at once in Jesus' name. We pled the blood of Jesus and His finished work on the cross over us and declared Him as our Lord and Master.

Immediately the atmosphere changed. I felt the fulfillment of Psalm 18:32, as if the Lord had armed me with His strength, and the heaviness of fear was replaced with great peace.

> *He sent out his arrows and scattered them ... .*
> *He rescued me from my strong enemy.*
> —Psalm 18:14 and 17

## FREE AT LAST

Shortly thereafter I struggled with terrible abdominal pain. I did not understand what was happening. I thought maybe I was coming down with something. What resulted produced a terrible pungent, horrible, death-laden odor. It was not human or earthly. Once expelled, my body settled down. I felt incredibly clean, light, joyous, and peaceful. My mind was sharp and clear, and my spirit was rejoicing in God my Savior.

What left? Pain, fear, insecurity, fatigue, impatience, striving. I even thought perhaps my old nature had died. It didn't matter. I was so thankful and I was free at last!

Many Christians have been taught that they cannot have a demon if they are truly saved. This belief was carefully considered by C. Fred Dickason, Th.D., an authority on angelology and the spirit world. I recommend reading his books: *De-*

*mon Possession and the Christian* [3] and *Angels: Elect and Evil.* [4] It is my firm belief (and this has been confirmed by many in various mission fields), that Christians can be demonized, and their bodies can be attacked by dark forces—even though they are saved and baptized in the Holy Spirit. Any type of sin, known or unknown—from unbelief to being double-minded, like confessing symptoms instead of resisting and taking authority over them—can give the devil a foothold. We must always resist the devil and his evil schemes. To not resist him is to give him the foothold he so desires.

A deep and abiding love for the Lord God will lead you to desire to be free of all darkness, including sickness, disease, and addictions. These are all hindrances in your walk and intimacy with God. The Holy Spirit wants to dwell in a temple that is completely holy. Your body is the Outer Court of the Temple and needs to be cleansed, just as surely as Christ Himself cleansed the Outer Court of the physical Temple in His day.

Jesus healed a demonized boy His disciples could not heal. Then He scolded the people for being faithless. The father of the boy cried out and asked Jesus to help. He said, *"If you can ..."* (Mark 9:22). Jesus responded:

---

3. Chicago, Illinois, Moody Publishers: 1975
4. Ibid

*All things are possible for one who believes.*
—Mark 9:23

The famous Reverend C.H. Spurgeon preached: *unbelief is the doubting of the promises of God:*

> *Unbelief took the form of a doubt of the divine veracity, or a mistrust of God's power. Either he doubted whether God really meant what he said, or whether it was within the range of possibility that God should fulfill his promise. Unbelief hath more phases than the moon, and more colors than the chameleon. Common people say of the devil, that he is seen sometimes in one shape, and sometimes in another. I am sure this is true of Satan's first-born child—unbelief, for its forms are legion.* [5]

Far too many Christians walk in unbelief concerning physical healing and deliverance.

- Living a life of true faith is having a positive response to all of God's Word and promises.
- We receive the promises fully, grow in faith,

5. "The Sin of Unbelief," No. 3, Delivered on Sabbath Morning, January 14, 1855, found at http://www.ccel.org/ccel/spurgeon/sermons01.iii.html

and make active our faith by doing what God says.

- We do not beg but, rather, thank God for what He has already done.
- If we cooperate with His promises, we will be victorious.
- We agree with God and approach Him based only on the righteousness of Christ and nothing else.
- We must use the authority Christ has given us over darkness, resist evil, and choose the good.

I believe that I became ensnared because of my own confessions. I did not think of an injury originating from a spirit being. I was living my life in the natural world, believing what the doctors said about me, instead of believing what God's Word says about me. I was not attuned enough to His promises. Although I believed Jesus was my Healer, my confessions and actions were lining up with the world instead of with God's Word.

Our words will either work for us or against us. Even in my weakened state, I made a decision to change my mindset.

## Living a Supernatural Lifestyle

For me, this was the beginning of living a sustained supernatural lifestyle. It was the beginning of full surrender. My time was no longer my own. I surrendered my time to the Lord and gave it a new definition:

**T** – TO
**I** – INCLINE
**M** – MY
**E** – EVERYTHING TO HIM

I am going to call this the "benefit of first things." We demonstrate our love to God by placing Him first in everything. The first thing in the morning we are to pray, the first day of the week we are to worship in community, and we offer to Him our firstfruits (the first portion of anything we have produced).

Here is one example of the benefit of placing God first:

One day I had the most unique experience in the wee hours of the morning before dawn. I woke up hearing the sound of an owl hooting right outside the glass doors of my bedroom. Its sound was beautiful and clear, and I knew its visit was very special.

On another day, about the same time in the darkness of early morning, I heard a bird cooing. It sounded like a dove. Its pecking on the same glass doors of my bedroom woke me. I never saw either the owl or the dove; I only heard their beautiful sounds. They were gone by the time I reached the door to see them. I realized Heaven was calling me to awaken from my slumber to spend time with my Beloved, Jesus. Every day I was awakened in some way.

On several occasions I received a wakeup call from alarm companies who had called me mistakenly at 3 A.M. I was also awakened by flood lights shining into my room. Various modes of wake-up began to occur at 3:33 or 4:44 AM, until I eventually began to wake up on my own, just by listening to the Holy Spirit's call. I obeyed the call, and through so doing, God was preparing something for me more magnificent than I could have imagined.

He said:

*Behold, I will do a new thing; now it shall spring forth; shall ye not know it? I will even make a way in the wilderness, and rivers in the desert. The beast of the field shall honour me, the dragons and the owls: because I give waters in the wilderness, and rivers in the desert, to give drink to my people, my chosen.*

—Isaiah 43:19-20, KJV

God made a way for His people Israel in the desert, and He gave them drink out of a rock. That rock was a representation of Jesus Christ, and the water was a representation of the Holy Spirit. We stand on the Rock of Christ and drink of the waters of the Holy Spirit.

God makes a way for us too. He made a way for me to walk in healing and wholeness. Before I was healed, however, He gave me a deeper desire for Him, and it began with prayer. Whatever your need is, remember: God is making a way especially and uniquely for you. In the wilderness AND in the desert, there is provision for life and blessing.

God is making a way to prepare us for His second coming. I believe God sent me two birds from Heaven and uniquely filled me with His light to signal important changes that are about to take place in the Church. The prophetic dispensation in these last days is as the owl, the dove, and the glory light.

God is making a way for the last-days Church to walk in greater revelation. Prophets and seers will operate at a higher spiritual level now, possessing supernatural hearing and sight like an owl. They will see things they've never seen before (like the owl who flies in the dark), and hear things they've never heard before (having the owl's sharp hearing). In this season, they will stop perching and yield to the wind of the Holy Spirit (dove) with greater trust and security. Their ministry to the Church will result in the Church possessing greater wisdom, insight, and virtue. The Holy Spirit will give us greater revelation.

We recognize the dove as a representative of the Holy Spirit, the third person of the Godhead, as He descended from Heaven at our Lord's baptism (see Matthew 3:16, Mark 1:10, Luke 3:22 and John 1:32). At Pentecost, the Holy Spirit also came to fill and impart heavenly gifts to believers in Christ (see Acts 2:1-4). It is especially important in this season that every Christian receive, know, and operate in the gift or gifts the Holy Spirit has given them. We must pray for the Church to be open to the gifts of the Holy Spirit operating now just as in the first-century Church.

A dove likes to eat seed and does *not* eat dead things, like the raven or crow, so the dove is said to represent purity. Jesus told His followers, in Matthew 10:16, to be *"innocent as doves."* In this representation we must model purity and innocence and turn our lives and eyes away from worthless things (see Psalm 119:37). Those who are devoted to Christ and desire His full stature will adhere to a life that becomes very narrow. They will be greatly empowered by their sacrifices and desire for His purity.

Most birds have wings that reach to their tails, and they tuck their wings behind them. But a dove's wings fold outward and forward toward the head. This represents our surrender and submission to the Most High God. Jesus Christ is the Head, and we are His Body. The last-days Church must be fully surrendered to Christ.

The dove is said to mount up to high places that are solitary, like the entrance of caves. This symbolizes our drawing away and gazing upon our Lord, our Creator and Redeemer, in the high places. We see in the life of Christ that He often drew away to solitary places to talk with the Father. As we model Christ and draw away from our daily activities, to spend time with Him, He will take us up in the high places of His Kingdom for divine impartation and purposes. We need a greater anointing and power of the Holy Spirit to counter the world's darkness.

Doves are peaceful, and they are calm and gentle companions. Mature Christians, in these last days, will be like doves—peaceful, calm, and gentle. Those who are peaceful in the midst of the shaking of the nations will be magnets to the demonized, unsaved, lost, and hurting people. There will be many who will be desperately searching for a place of safety. Peter wrote:

*Let your adorning be the hidden person of the heart with the imperishable beauty of a gentle and quiet spirit, which in God's sight is very precious.*

—1 Peter 3:4

How wonderful it is to be awakened with the sun's light! God wakes us up with the sun's light as though saying to all His creation, *"I want you to be like Me!"* Yet His light shines so much brighter than the sun. I believe God is telling us that, in these last days, He will shine in us greatly, and others will see His light in us. In this way, God will cause others to be drawn to us, giving us an opportunity to share our faith, and thereby expand His Kingdom on the earth.

Because God is love, we have love living on the inside of us. Love is very attractive to a world living in darkness, to those who live life without Christ. Remember, Christ went into places of spiritual darkness and shined His light there. His ministry began after He proclaimed He was the Light of the World.

*The people dwelling in darkness have seen a great light.*
—Matthew 4:16

God has called us to go and learn how to minister to people who do not have this light. During
these last days of the earth we must shine His light
into the spiritual darkness and moral bankruptcy
of this world. Let us pray for more light and receive the revelations and secret things God wants
to share with us. Let us increase His light in us (see
Reference 7, "Declarations of the Glory Light.")

*Light shines in the darkness for the godly.*
—Psalm 112:4, NLT

## A HOLY VISITATION

*Very early in the morning, while it was still dark,*
*Jesus got up, left the house and went off to a soli-*
*tary place, where he prayed.*
                              —Mark 1:35, NIV

Then one day, in the early morning preceding
dawn, as I prayed I was startled by a loud noise of
shuffling that sounded like it was coming from the
roof of my house, partly inside and partly outside.
The house literally shook. It trembled. I reasoned,
"Was that an earthquake?"

*Then the earth shook and trembled.*
                              —Psalm 18:7, KJV

I felt peaceful, yet on high spiritual alert, as I was
processing what was happening. I remember thinking that something or someone GREAT had just entered my room. Maybe a strong and mighty angel
had been sitting on my roof, a messenger with a message for me. I kept scanning the room and looking
around me. When I didn't see anything appear, I became concerned and started spiritual battle prayers.

Then I heard clearly in my right ear: "Lucy,
it's Me. Lucy, I know everything about you. Your

mother is Judith, and your father is Frank." I suddenly recognized the voice of my Savior Jesus, and I understood He was right there beside me—even though I could not see Him. I was in awe!

"He is here! He is here, in my house and *literally* talking to me outside of my body! He heard my prayers and praise and is answering my call to come and visit me! WOW!"

> *Come and listen, all who fear God and I will tell you what He did for me. For I cried out to him for help, praising him as I spoke.*
> —Psalm 66:16-17, NLT

My flesh could feel the closeness of the Lord. Greater peace and joy than I had ever known flooded my soul! Oh, how I love Him!

> *Arise, shine; for your light has come, and the glory of the LORD has risen upon you. For behold, darkness will cover the earth, and deep darkness the peoples; but the LORD will arise upon you, and his glory will be seen upon you.*
> —Isaiah 60:1-2

Days later, about three in the morning, while praying I felt the whole Person, the fullness of the

Holy Spirit enter my body. He descended into me, and I felt the thrust of His descending. His full stature entered and settled into me.

> *The Spirit of the LORD clothed Gideon…*
> —Judges 6:34

His lavish presence fit me like a glove. I could feel Him moving back and forth like one would fit their hand into a glove until it fits comfortably.

Immediately, I was completely filled with blazing and dazzling LIGHT—light that appeared brighter than the sun. I could feel and see the brilliant light coming through the opening of my eyes in the darkness of my room. With my eyes closed, I could see the light in a color of deep blue sapphire. My spirit rejoiced with great praise and worship. No one stands in the presence of the Almighty Spirit without an offering (see Deuteronomy 16:16, MSG). I was literally rejoicing all day and all night in God my Savior.

In my spirit I heard praise and worship every minute, every hour, and every day and recognized my own voice as the worshiper. What was extraordinary about this was that somehow the voice I heard was beautiful and perfect in tone, and quality, and it was on key.

I recognized the worship as songs I had sung to the Lord continually and perhaps over an entire lifetime. It was as though every sound of praise I had ever offered had risen to Heaven and been received, then captured and fine-tuned by an audio engineer, and then downloaded back to me as a masterpiece of worship.

In a moment He changed my body, inhabited fully by His glorious body (see Philippians 3:20-21), and I was encapsulated by the bread of His presence (see Exodus 25:23-30), as He stood in the midst of the gift of praise. The Temple where the Jews worshiped contained a table with bread that was called the showbread, or the bread of His presence. This bread represented the display of perpetual thank offerings to God for His many blessings.

In the New Testament, Jesus Christ is the fulfillment of the Temple showbread, or the *"bread of life"* (John 6:35), to whom we offer perpetual praise.

I was filled with great wonder and awe of God, and He had my full attention, as though time had stopped. He was my only thought. I had no personal desires of any kind other than Him. There was no desire to speak or to reason, and I did not want to say or do anything except please Him. Soaking His presence into my soul, spirit, and body was immeasurably wonderful.

I was completely undone by all of this, swept away. There was no fear, no questions, and no explanations needed. NOTHING else mattered except hosting and enjoying my blessed Redeemer.

The Spirit had given me a song years earlier, and now it suddenly became my reality:

*I seek nothing, Lord,*
*but just being in Your presence.*
*I seek nothing, Lord,*
*but just being in Your presence.*
*In Your presence is blessing and joy.*
*In Your presence is peace and righteousness.*

My eyes have seen the beauty and splendor of my King, and I hope this changes your perception of God. The Holy Spirit is the most loving, gentle, kind, patient, tender Person ever. He is so sweet. He is so intelligent. He is filled with glory, and He knows everything. I cry my eyes out as I realize how I fall so short in expressing how wonderful the Spirit of the Most High is!

The fullness of the Holy Spirit was living and moving inside of me and He stayed with me for three weeks. My life was worship, praise, and prayer, while still living a human existence through pure necessity. I was quite literally feeling Him moving in my body every day. He looked through my eyes.

On Sunday, when we entered to worship with our congregation, I could feel Him dancing and jumping inside me every time scriptures were read and during exuberant praise and worship. I was reminded of John the Baptist leaping in his mother's womb in Luke 1:41, as he was filled with the Holy Spirit, and I wondered if Elizabeth had shared my experience.

During one particular Sunday church service a woman came up to me in the dim light of the sanctuary and, facing me, took both my hands and stared for a long time into my face. She wondered why I looked so different, why my face seemed to shine. It was not easy to explain.

The Holy Spirit is filled with great compassion and great power. During this holy visitation from Him, every person I prayed for immediately received healing. He impressed upon me the power of our tongue and the need for wisdom, temperance, reservation, and restraint. Then, it seemed, as suddenly as He had arrived, I felt His departure.

It happened one morning, as I was walking down a hallway in our house. Suddenly I felt Him leap out of my body and could feel the thrust of His powerful departure. He quickly arose, and I heard

Him pronounce many divine and great proclama-
tions—things I had never heard before (and was
not permitted to retain).

My mind cannot reconcile how I can still be
talking with Him daily and hearing from Him. He
is still by my side, living in me. I can physically feel
His presence and power rise up on my side, like a
bubbling brook. I feel His powerful presence in my
body when I worship, when I pray, when I minister (as in Mark 16:17-18), when I say a particular
person's name, or when I have a particular encoun-
ter. On one occasion when I touched someone, they
felt the physical manifestation of the Holy Spirit's
presence, and power enter their body through their
hands and up their arms and went into their heart!

I believe God answers all my prayers. He continues to awaken me every morning to spend time
with Him. Even though I sleep less, I never feel
tired. My communion with the Holy Spirit always
results in being energized.

Now His presence was transformed magnif-
icently. I reconciled His departure with the story
of Jesus' transfiguration recorded in the Scriptures
recorded in Matthew 17:2-8 and Mark 9:2-8. When
our Lord was transfigured, His disciples—Peter, James, and John—were present. It is written
that while our Lord was praying, His appearance

changed, and in the bewilderment of the moment, Peter expressed human understanding, and suddenly the transfiguration disappeared, and the appearance of Christ returned to human form.

Christ did not leave them, but His presence was transformed. *That transfiguration was the assurance of the future Messianic Age.* This age will be characterized by righteousness, justice, and peace; by the outpouring of the Holy Spirit; and by the restoration and renewal of God's people and of creation. In the Messianic Age, Christ will reign for one thousand years, and the kingdom of darkness will be fully bound.

That is the reason I have entitled this book *The Anointing Preceding the Messianic Age.* I feel so strongly about the soon coming of Christ to rule and reign on the earth but also so strongly about the expectation of a great outpouring of the Holy Spirit upon all flesh. And, I believe, this outpouring will precede the Messianic Age.

During this last outpouring, the Body of Christ will experience the miracles represented by Aaron's staff. Symbolically, the staff was the arm of God reflected in His perfect Son, Jesus Christ. The full spiritual equipping of the saints will continue ...

*Until all attain to the unity of the faith and of the knowledge of the Son of God, to mature man-*

*hood, to the measure of the stature of the fullness of Christ.*

*—*Ephesians 4:13

Aaron's staff was a sign of God's miraculous power. The staff was full of buds, blossoms, and fruit—all at the same time. What was the fruit? It was almonds. Almonds are the first among all trees to awaken the spring.

Aaron was a priest under the Old Covenant. Believers (we) are priests under the New Covenant. Our staff today is the Holy Spirit Who co-labors with us to accomplish the miraculous, to glorify Christ."

## THE AWAKENING AND THE FEASTS

This awakening speaks of the feasts of the Lord or the order of things. Greater revelation is available to the saints as we study God's feast days. Here is a short summary:

- Christ fulfilled the spring feasts of Israel. These feasts were dress rehearsals for His first coming.
- The first feast was Passover. Christ was the perfect Passover Lamb, crucified as

the Lamb of God who took away the sins
of the world (see John 1:29).

- Christ then fulfilled the second feast:
The Feast of Unleavened Bread. He was
the Bread of God who came down from
Heaven (our manna from Heaven), and
those who eat of this Bread will never die
(see John 6:31-40). This is represented in
our Communion supper.

- Christ fulfilled the Feast of First Fruits
by rising from the dead and promising
those who believe in Him everlasting life
(see John 3:16) and a future *resurrection*
(see 1 Thessalonians 4:16-17).

- Fifty days later Christ fulfilled the Feast
of Shavuot, or Pentecost, when the Holy
Spirit of Promise was poured out on the
Body of Christ with flames of fire from
our God, who is an all-consuming fire
(see Act 2:1-4). The Holy Spirit was giv-
en to empower the saints to do the work
of the Kingdom of God on the earth (see
Acts 1:8).

Now we await the fulfillment of the fall feasts,
which are Israel's dress rehearsals for Christ's second coming. The Feast of Trumpets (representing

repentance), the Feast of Yom Kippur (representing redemption) and the Feast of Tabernacles, also called the Messianic Age or Millennial Age (representing rejoicing). The Messianic Age will be a time when all nations will celebrate the King of kings' one-world government on the earth!

Christ fulfilled the spring feasts very quickly, and I believe this order of things will continue, with Christ fulfilling the fall feasts quickly as well. I also believe that the Church will fulfill God's mandate to inherit the full measure of Christ preceding the Messianic Age. Personally I experienced the fullness of Christ during the holy visitation I shared with you already in this book. It is our intimacy with Christ that causes us to live and operate in God's supernatural realm, or, as some would say, being in the glory zone or under an open Heaven.

Heaven's culture is not constrained by time. Aaron's staff was not constrained by time. I believe this is a word from the Lord that signs of spiritual gifts and energies will appear with ripened fruit not constrained by time. As the Lord continues to bring His saints into maturity and into the fullness of Christ, may it be recorded as a time of great repentance.

His glorious presence continues in me. He imparts gifts and revelations. I speak to Him with reverence. I tell Him how much I love Him and how He is my Best Friend. I say "good morning" to Him and "good night" to Him. He tells me things before they happen. He leads me to people He wants me to speak to. When I pray for them, they'll respond, "You were reading my mind."

On special occasions, my whole body will tingle, like a light switching on, and I can feel transference of energy rising up and encompassing me. He daily awakens me, and my soul rejoices with praise, as I feel the internal heat of His indwelling light and power. I can still see His light flare up with my eyes closed, when I passionately worship, pray in the Spirit, sing in the Spirit, pray with understanding, read the Bible, or loudly declare His Word.

At times He gives me a word, a vision, a word of knowledge, an interpretation of a dream, a scripture reference, a prophetic utterance, or instructions. One thing is certain: every day with the Holy Spirit is an exciting and fun day.

One evening I was talking to Him, of how much I missed seeing His full brilliant light shining through my eyes, and I began to weep. I love Him so much. Being one with Him is my greatest quest and desire.

This is a love that cannot be explained in human terms. He is my breath; He is my life; He is the reason for my existence, for my being. He is my purpose, my greatest pleasure, and my greatest passion. I can identify with Mary Magdalene's passion, as she was clinging to Jesus, not wanting to let Him go (see John 20:16-17).

One day I heard the Holy Spirit say, "Second Corinthians 5:4," so I looked up the passage:

> *While we live in this earthly tent, we groan with a feeling of oppression; it is not that we want to get rid of our earthly body, but that we want to have the heavenly one put on over us, so that what is mortal will be transformed by life. God is the one who has prepared us for this change, and he gave us his Spirit as the guarantee of all that he has in store for us. So we are always full of courage. We know that as long as we are at home in the body we are away from the Lord's home.*
>
> —2 Corinthians 5:4-6, GNT

I was home in the body, longing to be transformed. I remembered the days of struggling with pain in my whole body. There was not a place on my body that did not hurt. But step-by-step the Lord restored me. I confessed healing and strength to each area of my body. I prayed for the Holy Spirit to go into any area I was having a problem with, and He made me whole.

Now every single day I tell Him:

*Thank You, King Jesus, for surrendering Your body and Your blood to give me eternal life. Thank You for giving me Your Holy Spirit. Thank You for healing me and making me whole. Thank You for Your living Word and Your eternal love and grace.*

I had experienced major improvements in my physical condition through an anointed healing minister. Then, praise God, when the fullness of the Holy Spirit entered my body, all fatigue left, and I was filled with divine energy and with fruit abounding! What a miracle!

# CHAPTER 6

# Light That Bears Fruit

---

**It is good to give thanks to the Lord, to sing praises to the Most High. It is good to proclaim your unfailing love in the morning, your faithfulness in the evening.**

—Psalm 92:1-2, NLT

PASTOR ANNA VISITED AGAIN FROM Korea, and I offered my home for a healing meeting. I thought about all the cleaning and de-cluttering we would need to do. In the meantime, we were keeping her visit in our prayers and inviting people to the meetings.

On more than one occasion, upon awaking, I was praying in the Spirit and, in my mind's eye, I would see a sinister laughing face, almost like a fat clown face. On one occasion, I woke up with the words flashing in my mind, "BLACK WID-

OW! BLACK WIDOW!" My initial reaction was to shine my flashlight across the floor to see if there was a spider there. I asked the Holy Spirit what it meant but could not discern an answer. I shared the visions and this warning with Rich, telling him that I sensed it was not about an actual insect, a spider, but there was something about a spider we needed to know. Then I asked him, "What do we need to know about a spider?"

He answered, "It is something that is hidden." Some days later he said to me, "Guess what I found?" The Holy Spirit had directed him to an old box in our basement, being stored there by a family member. We had no idea what was inside. When he opened it, he found a Buddha ceramic that was actually used to burn incense. He smashed it and threw it in the trash.

Ceramics like these are all over America, and you can see them in Asian restaurants. He later said the image had a fat face, almost like a clown, and that was the image I had been receiving. It is a breaking of the first commandment to have anything in our possession that represents an idol. It gives the devil a legal right to access. Remember, if we do not resist evil, we are condoning it. To *condone* is "to disregard, accept, allow, let pass, turn a blind eye to, overlook, forget, forgive, pardon, excuse, and/or to let go." This experience gave me a greater sensitivity to the Holy Spirit. Ask Him if there is anything that needs to be removed from your person, your home, or your church. I believe He will show you any obstacle to His presence.

Praise be to God! Our God is awesome and the light of His Holy Spirit reveals darkness and cleanses us. The meeting with Pastor Anna went as planned, with no obstacles, and many people received healing through the laying on of her hands and her prayers. She instructed us that God wants His Church to be dedicated to praying in the Spirit (see Ephesians 6:18). She said we are living in very difficult times before Christ's return, and by praying in the Spirit we are slaying the enemies of God in the spirit realm.

We were also encouraged to pray for God's strength and protection:

> *Keep awake then and watch at all times [be discreet, attentive, and ready], praying that you may have the full strength and ability and be accounted worthy to escape all these things [taken together] that will take place, and to stand in the presence of the Son of Man.*
>
> —Luke 21:36, AMP

When we yield ourselves to the Holy Spirit to live in Heaven's culture, this transforms our environment through the love and power of God.

In a recent supernatural living conference attended by about sixty-five people (strangers from all over the country), we made active our faith and gifts from the Holy Spirit with words of knowledge on healing. The instructor prayed and asked God to show us each something about another person in the room who was seeking help or healing. One-by-one the participants began having some type of manifestation of what another person was feeling, and each one stepped out in faith and declared the word of knowledge. Then an invitation was made for anyone with that particular malady to step forward for prayer. Many people were healed, and one made a confession of salvation. Praise God!

During the prayer, I saw, with my eyes closed, a dark vision, with a ghost coming forward from a distance, and I knew that someone named Charles was going through a spooky time in his life and needed help. We announced the word of knowledge, and one of the participants jumped up shouting, "That's for my son! That's for my son!" A group of women at her table stood up in amazement. Everything I had said was what they had been talking about an hour earlier during lunch. The Holy Spirit had spoken through me to minister confirmation, healing, and deliverance.

In the natural, I had no idea what I was doing. I simply yielded to the Spirit, and He used every detail, bringing a beautiful symphony of light where there had been darkness. Praise be to God! Praise and glory to the Father, King Jesus, and His Holy Spirit!

This is the season. This is the time for the Body of Christ to come into full maturity. It's time for all believers to live a supernatural lifestyle. It's time for the Bride to prepare herself. It's time for the full stature of the Bride to meet her Bridegroom.

Jesus promised He would return and, with the sounding of a trumpet, He would lift up, or catch away, His Bride from the earth. The English translation for "catching away" is *rapture.* This truth is based on 1 Thessalonians 4:14-18. Christ will come for His Bride to bring her to Himself for the Marriage Supper of the Lamb (see Revelation 19:9) and, in the process, to protect her and provide a way of escape for her from the terrible things that will begin to happen on the earth once she has been removed.

Jesus' Bride is said to be *"without spot or wrinkle"* (Ephesians 5:27). *Without spot* represents holiness. *Without wrinkle,* or without a blemish, represents physical, as well as spiritual wholeness. The word translated *wrinkle* in the Greek is *rhutis*, meaning "no mark or decay." This word is commonly applied to body wrinkles, indicative of sickness. The flesh manifests the spirit (see Leviticus 13:2).

This mystery is similar to the Israelites being called out of Egyptian slavery to worship their Hebrew God. He had prepared a place for them, a place called the Promised Land. When the Israelites left Egypt, it is written, *"There was not one feeble person among their tribes"* (Psalm 105:37, KJV). The English Standard Version of the Bible describes the Israelites' condition as: *"none among his tribes who stumbled,"* implying that they were strengthened and made physically whole as they departed.

Believers in Christ have been given *"all authority in heaven and on the earth"* (Matthew 28:18) and an invitation to be FULL of the Holy Spirit (see Acts 1:8). We are encouraged to pursue love and earnestly seek spiritual gifts (see 1 Corinthians 14:1). We have been given precious promises from our heavenly Father. As we yield ourselves and press into King Jesus and His heavenly realm, we will realize an increase of His Spirit's light.

Today we are seeing a Holy Spirit outpouring upon the nations where the church is being persecuted and the Great Commission of winning souls to Christ is being realized with signs and wonders following His disciples.

Believers who have received ALL Jesus died to give them will come into maturity, operating under the anointing of the fullness of God. I believe the maturity of the Body of Christ in the world will result in the end-time harvest of souls and powerful manifestations of the Holy Spirit. The collective power of the Holy Spirit working through millions of mature believers will shake the world in the greatest magnitude, beyond what was experienced by the first-century church. To God be the glory!

# PART III

# Essential References

# Understanding the Anointing

THE NEW TESTAMENT GREEK WORDS translated *anoint* are *chrio*, which means "to smear or rub with oil" implying, "to consecrate for office or religious service" and *aleipho*, which means "to anoint." In Bible times people were anointed with oil to signify God's blessing or call on their life. They were also anointed for special purposes, such as becoming a king, a prophet, or for some other gifting (see Exodus 29:7 and 40:13, 2 Kings 9:6, Ecclesiastes 9:8, James 5:14 and 1 Samuel 16:13).

Anointing is a symbol of being blessed, protected, and empowered. Anointing someone may mean covering with a cosmetic, as in the story of Esther, or literally invoking the power of God upon a person. The oil itself has no power and should not be viewed as some kind of magic liquid. Only God can anoint a person for a specific purpose.

The church was to use oil as a symbol to confirm what God was doing or to align with the practice of anointing used by leaders to impart healing to those who were sick (see Mark 6:13). Anointing with oil was also used to prepare Jesus for burial (see Mark 14:8).

Another meaning of being anointed is being "chosen." Jesus Christ was anointed by God with the Holy Spirit to spread the Good News and to free those held under the power of sin (see Luke 4:18-19 and Acts 10:38). After Christ's resurrection, His followers were given the gift of the Holy Spirit (see 3 John 14:16, Acts 1:4-5 and Acts 2:2-4).

All believers in Christ have been anointed (see 1 John 2:20). We have been given incredible promises as those "chosen." Here are a few of them:

*Whoever believes in me shall never thirst.*
—John 6:35

*Out of his heart will flow rivers of living water.*
—John 7:38

*Though he die, yet shall he live.*
—John 11:25

When we examine the New Testament, we see the effects of being "anointed" with the Holy Spirit. The apostles and disciples demonstrated manifestations of the Holy Spirit by living devout lives as worshipers of Christ with a deep desire to share His goodness with others. They shared what they had been taught, imitating the Master in taking authority over demons, imparting healing to the sick, and with various other signs, wonders, and miracles following them.

We can pray for the anointing and/or be prayed for to receive the anointing of the Holy Spirit. We can also receive greater measures of the Holy Spirit's anointing as we see happening in the life of Elijah and others. We can also lose the anointing based on disobedience, as did King Saul (see 1 Samuel 16:14) or walk in a greater anointing of the Holy Spirit through our love, obedience, and faithfulness to God. We are to live a life of earnestly seeking Christ. He is the Anointed One and has an unlimited portion of the anointing of God. Therefore seek more of Him:

> *Earnestly desire and zealously cultivate the greatest and best gifts and graces (the higher gifts and the choicest graces).*
> —1 Corinthians 12:31, AMP

# Healing Anticipation

---

**A man can receive nothing, except it be given him from heaven.**
—John 3:27, KJV

ALL YOU NEED TO BE HEALED IS FAITH in Jesus. There are testimonies of Christians going into foreign nations and, on a little platform, declaring who Jesus is, what He did, and what He said. They promised: "His Word is truth and He cannot lie" (see John 17:17 and Titus 1:2, KJV). They didn't have anything else, such as worship music or worldly, fancy presentations. They simply stood on God's promises. Still, when they had declared the Word and prayed, people were healed and delivered.

This appendix simply shares my experience of anticipating healing. May you, dear Christian, align with Heaven's perspective.

1. Have a change of attitude. Jesus taught us to forgive. We must forgive everyone who has ever offended us. Let it go!

2. Clear all distractions and desire to be healed! My attitude changed from moaning about how terrible I was feeling to being grateful and thankful. I replaced a pain diary with a spiritual journal. My intent was to journal progress toward healing in the pain diary, but the effect was the opposite. The spiritual journal turned my focus entirely on Jesus. It began with a simple entry that has grown into hundreds of encouraging, faith-building expectations that then turned into reality.

3. Be Spirit led. Act and obey the directions of the Holy Spirit. Pray for discernment and wisdom to hear His voice. Trust and expect God to answer. Wait, listen, and yield to release His anointing upon you.

4. Offer regular and continuous praise to God:

*Blessed are the people who know the passwords of praise, who shout on parade in the bright presence of GOD.*

—Psalm 89:15, MSG

Everyone who enters God's presence will

praise Him. They know the Lord and cannot keep silent. They offer Him abundant praise. Praise is a gift we give our God. We have been given the password to unlock and open the gates of Heaven with our praise, because it is God Himself who inhabits the praises of His people. When praises go up to Heaven, blessings come down. King David said we are to enter His gates with thanksgiving and enter His courts with PRAISE (see Psalm 100:4).

God wants us to lift up holy hands to Him (see Psalm 134:2, NLT) and worship according to His Word. Let us imitate the worship of Aaron, Moses, King David, King Solomon, Ezra, and the people of Israel, as they lifted up holy hands in prayer and worship to Him who is King of all nations.

Hands lifted up is an admission of our surrender and dependence upon God, just as a child is dependent upon a parent and lifts up their hands to be cuddled or carried (see Psalm 63:4, Isaiah 1:15-17, Exodus 9:29, 1 Kings 8:22 and 54, Nehemiah 8:6 and 1 Timothy 2:8).

*"Shout to God with a voice of triumph"* (Psalm 47:1, AMPC), thanking Him for the answer

to our petition just as if it had already manifested and dancing as though the victory is won. This is a working of our faith.

Worship God by revering His name. In Malachi 3:16, we read about a book, or scroll, of remembrance:

*Then those who feared the LORD spoke with each other, and the LORD listened to what they said. In his presence, a scroll of remembrance was written to record the names of those who feared him and always thought about the honor of his name.* (NLT)

5. Invite the Holy Spirit into YOU, your home, your family, your church. His presence will manifest as we offer sacrifices of praise and worship (see Ezra 3:3), then He will transform our bodies into temples of worship.

6. Read, confess and pray God's promises (see Proverbs 13:2). Read the Bible out loud: *"Faith comes from hearing, and hearing through the word of Christ"* (Romans 10:17). Read Christian books on the power of the tongue and the authority of the believer. Speak positively about the problem area (your body, the relationship, your finances, etc.). Bless,

in His name, every part of your body and dedicate it to His service.

7. Fast and pray to drive out natural *"unbelief"* (Matthew 17:20-21).

8. Learn who you are in Christ and confess His authority over the fallen one, the spiritual world, and the natural world. Submit yourself to God, resist the devil, and he will flee (see James 4:7). I told the fallen one to leave ... until I felt him leave. I commanded the lying symptoms to leave ... until they did. I envisioned myself as God saw me: anointed, healed, peaceful, and whole.

9. Ask for prayer and pray for others to be healed following the spiritual principle of sowing and reaping (see James 5:16 and Galatians 6:8). Pray for your soul to prosper (see 3 John 1:2, AMPC). My new confession over those who need healing is this: "Jesus suffered for your healing, and He deserves your healing." Healing was provided by Jesus on the cross, just as salvation was provided by Jesus. We need to learn how to receive our healing, just as we receive our salvation.

10. Before all symptoms were gone, I took bold steps of faith.

# Healing Scriptures

CHRISTIANS CAN COME UNDER SPIRITU-
AL attack through sickness and disease. Its purpose may be to keep us weak and less of a threat to
the fallen one, thereby delaying the advancement
of God's destiny for you or delaying the advancement of His Kingdom on the earth. Sickness and
disease may also be the result of ours or another's
poor choices or disobedience to God's instructions
(see John 5:14).

Jesus taught us to pray the Lord's Prayer that
Heaven would be on the earth. There is no sickness
in Heaven, and we are to receive what Jesus did
for us on the cross. By His stripes we are healed
(see Isaiah 53:5). Jesus demonstrated that He can
heal any sickness and any disease. Christians have
a legal right to wholeness because Jesus Christ
paid for it with His very own body and blood. In

contrast, Jesus could not do many miracles in His hometown because of the sin of unbelief (see Matthew 13:57-58 and Mark 6:4-5).

We don't have to beg for healing. You'll never be good enough to receive healing, never holy enough. God did not use sickness and disease to teach me something; neither was my healing a personal validation of my acceptance with God. We receive our healing by exercising childlike faith. Christ has already provided your healing in His own body on the cross. Jesus paid it all, so He deserves your healing!

There are many healing scriptures in the Bible, in books on healing, and online. Find a handful that are meaningful for your situation and declare them out loud every day.

**Remember: your healing is based on Father God's relationship with Jesus Christ, His only Son in whom He is well pleased.**

Jesus paid it all! Jesus deserves your healing! You are healed by the unmerited favor of God upon you because you are in Christ.

I paraphrased and declared the following scriptures as prayers, day and night:

**Joshua 1:8**

*The Book of the Law shall not depart from my mouth. I will meditate on it day and night, I will observe to do according to all that is written in it, for then You will make my way prosperous and I will have good success, in the name of Jesus Christ.*

**Proverbs 4:20-22**

*I attend to Your Word God. I incline my ears to Your sayings. I will not let Your Word depart from my eyes. I will keep Your sayings in the midst of my heart for I have found them and they are LIFE to me and HEALTH to ALL my flesh, in the name of Jesus Christ.*

**Isaiah 55:11**

*I believe all of Your Word, God, that came out of Your mouth; it is LIFE to me and prospers in me, in the name of Jesus Christ.*

**Matthew 21:22**

*I really believe I will receive whatever I ask for in prayer in the name of Jesus Christ.*

**Isaiah 53:5**

*Jesus Christ was bruised for my iniquities … . And by His stripes I am healed.*

## Psalm 103:1-3

*Bless the Lord, O my soul! In the name of Jesus Christ, I remember Your benefits.... . You heal all my disease (or any dis-ease).*

## Malachi 4:2

*As I revere your name, God, You have promised, the sun of righteousness will rise with healing in His wings, in the name of Jesus Christ.*

## Jeremiah 30:17

*My God will restore my health and heal my wounds, in the name of Jesus Christ!*

## Psalm 30:2

*Thank You, O Lord my God; I cried out to You and in the name of Jesus Christ, You healed me.*

# Standing in the Armor of God

---

THE CHRISTIAN LIFE IS NOT CENTERED on spiritual warfare; it is centered on our love for Christ. Our focus is on loving God and loving others, as embodied by what Jesus said were the two greatest commandments (see Matthew 22:37-40). The marks of a Christian are that our love is genuine and that we hold fast to that which is good (see Romans 12:9). Spiritual conflict is expected and inevitable as we stand up for what is right and do not passively compromise with sin.

The Church is now in the second decade of the twenty-first century. It has suffered persecution since its birth. Jesus said He would return during a time He said would be *"as the days of Noah"* (Matthew 24:37). Noah's days were like our days, characterized by great wickedness, a day when man's imagination and thoughts are continually evil (see Genesis 6:5).

Moses sang, *"The LORD is a warrior"* (Exodus 15:3, NIV). We recognize from the history of Israel's battles and the psalms, that praise is spiritual warfare. The followers of Christ are called soldiers. For such a time as this, we are exhorted to be strong in the Lord and be prepared for spiritual battles.

> *Finally, be strong in the Lord and in His mighty power. Put on the full armor of God so that you can take your stand against the devil's schemes.*
> —Ephesians 6:10-11, NIV

The enemy's schemes are deception, doubt, discouragement, diversion, division, delay, and defeat—everything that is evil and dark. We live in the Kingdom of Light, which overcomes darkness. Our God has an army in Heaven and an army on the earth as a hedge of protection available to every believer. We are here to advance His Kingdom on enemy territory. The battle we are engaged in is for the human heart and the struggle of who will be worshiped.

To be a soldier in God's army, one must be fully surrendered to His will: to believe on His Son, Jesus Christ and His Word and to allow the Holy Spirit to transform us into the likeness of Christ. We are supernaturally created beings, living a human experience. We must give our full allegiance to God the Father, the Son, and the Holy Spirit, to live the victorious and abundant life Jesus died to give us. We are fully equipped with the full armor of God and protected by angels.

The armor represents our intimacy and standing with God through Christ. We stand in the FULL armor of God by the infilling of the Holy Spirit (see Acts 1:8).

It is the Holy Spirit who empowers us to be victorious in battle (see 2 Chronicles 20:15 and Psalm 34:7, to name just two).

To receive Jesus Christ, pray:

*Father in Heaven,*

*I agree with You. I have done wrong in my thoughts, words, and deeds; and I am willing now to turn away from all wrongdoing. Please forgive me. I believe Jesus Christ personally carried the load of my sins in His own body when He died on the cross. Right now, I surrender my life to Jesus Christ and ask Him to come and live inside of me.*

*Amen!*

Many believers are not filled with the Holy Spirit. When the Holy Spirit comes upon you, you are going to have POWER. I'll say it again: you are going to have POWER. The Holy Spirit is FULL of POWER, and He wants to live on the inside of you. You can live a supernatural life of victory every day as you yield to the Holy Spirit. If you have received Jesus Christ as your Lord (Master) and Savior, ask God to cleanse you in body, soul, and spirit and ask the Holy Spirit to come and live inside of you, with the evidence of speaking a heavenly language.

### *The full or whole armor of God includes praying in the Spirit.*

This is our heavenly prayer language (see Ephesians 6:18 and 1 Corinthians 14:15). When we are speaking to God—through prayer, praising, singing, or magnifying Him—no human language interpretation is necessary, for He knows what the Spirit is speaking (see Romans 8:26-27 and 1 Corinthians 14:2). It is through praying with our spirit that the Holy Spirit works wonders, as we intercede for others and expand the Kingdom through a bold witness to the world while, at the same time, fighting demonic forces.

Our armor is made of light (see Romans 13:12), for Christ is the Light of the World (see John 8:12). Our earthen vessels hold a treasure trove of light and glory. This light is given to us through the Holy Spirit.

*The supernatural light abiding in us can be increased or decreased according to our decisions (see 1 John 1:7). We must be filled with God's light to stand in the day of battle.*

*The light shines in the darkness, and the darkness has not overcome it.*

—John 1:5

*Peace I leave with you.*

—John 14:27

Before Jesus was crucified, He told His disciples that the fallen one, *"the prince (evil genius, ruler) of this world"* was coming (John 14:30, AMP). But what He proclaims next is the most important truth and revelation to be embraced by every Christian who desires to live victoriously:

*… And he [the fallen one] has no claim on Me. [He has nothing in common with Me; there is nothing in Me that belongs to him, and he has no power over Me.]*

—John 14:30, AMP

Nothing, nothing, nothing! Christian, if you are not living a life of peace and love, then you are in a spiritual battle—whether it be mental, emotional, physical (sickness or disease), or relational—conflict or trauma. Examine yourself and ask God to examine you to ensure there is no darkness, nothing in common with the fallen one. If we live as children of the light, in His light, yielding to His light, there will be no foothold or commonality with darkness. It is in being fully enveloped in Christ's light that we will be victorious. We do not yield to darkness; we oppose it.

Let's look further at Christ's spiritual graces described in our armor and weapons, as stated in 2 Corinthians 10:3-4. Paul also outlines these in Ephesians 6:10-18:

## The Helmet of Salvation

The helmet of salvation is to protect the head, the brain, and our senses, which include hearing, seeing, smelling and taste. We are to walk in supernatural anointing by sharpening our senses (see Hebrews 5:14 AMP).

A mature believer's eyes will receive life from God's Word, their ears will hear His commands, and their nose will distinguish between good and evil. (We have experienced smelling evil and commanding it to leave, and we have smelled the sweetness of the Holy Spirit and angels in a room full of worshipers.)

Because *"death and life are in the power of our tongue"* (Proverbs 18:21), we use our words carefully.

The helmet is called salvation because *"we have the mind of Christ"* (1 Corinthians 2:16). We have set our minds and affections on things above, not on things of this earth (see Colossians 3:2). We love God with our mind (see Mark 12:30). Think about what we are doing with our mind. Yield your mind and fill it with good things, so it will be a place God wants to inhabit.

The helmet covering our brain and senses will pull down strongholds and destroy arguments and every high thing that exalts itself against the knowledge of God (see 2 Corinthians 10:3-6). We can be victorious in the battles fought in the mind.

## THE BREASTPLATE OF RIGHTEOUSNESS

Covering our hearts is our breastplate called righteousness. When we received Jesus as our Lord and Savior, we received the righteousness of God in Christ (see 2 Corinthians 5:21). We seek and do things His way (see Matthew 6:33). His righteousness covers our heart and soul and deflects all evil and every deception.

## THE BELT OF TRUTH

The belt of truth holds all of our apparel up. We wear Christ by our baptism in Him. In Galatians 3:27 (AMP), it says we have clothed ourselves with Christ. He is our apparel. The belt holds up our breastplate, His righteousness. The belt of truth is the person of Christ. He is the Truth, the Way, and the Life (see John 14:6).

## THE GOSPEL OF PEACE SHOES

Our feet represent our lifestyle—where we go and what we do. A soldier is able to stand with the right kind of shoes. We have been given the shoes of peace. We do not look for spiritual fights. We stand protected with the armor and use God's Word to defeat the enemy. We can stand confident because we trust and know God has already defeated our enemies and will place them under our feet (see Romans 16:20).

## THE SHIELD OF FAITH

The shield of faith is the size of a door. We can shut any door, any portal of darkness, by our confession (a holy lifestyle and declaring God's Word). This great shield represents Christ, who is the Door of our Salvation. He shields us from attacks of the enemy through His Word, through faith in the blood of Christ, and through the Holy Spirit. This door is our front guard and our rear guard and can protect our whole body. The shield is firmly strapped to our forearm, so it cannot be dropped. It is either in a resting position, or it is in a defensive position. Imagine your shield of faith has Christ's insignia mark on it, as the King of Kings, and is backed up by the army of Heaven. We never fight alone. We are one soldier in a mighty and innumerable army.

### THE SWORD OF THE SPIRIT

The sword of the Spirit rests in the sheath of the belt. If we follow the truth (Jesus Christ and His teachings of right living), we will always have ready access to the sword, which is our main defensive weapon in spiritual warfare. This sword is by our side, and the Spirit of Christ is on our side (see Psalm 16:8), ever with us, never leaving us. The world is unaware of the fact that we are packing heat and carrying a concealed weapon every day.

Whenever we hear anything connected to the Spirit, we know it has life. Matthew 10:34 describes the sword as having a dividing effect. The sword has a double edge. One side of the sword is symbolic of THE WRITTEN WORD OF GOD (Greek *logos*); the other edge is THE SPOKEN WORD (Greek *rhema*).

Christ spoke the Word in His desert temptation to defeat the enemy (see Matthew 4:1-11).

In Saint John's vision, we see Christ in Heaven with a sharp two-edged sword coming out of His mouth (see Revelation 1:16).

Our sword is sharpened on the Rock of our Salvation, as we study His Word and hide it in our hearts. We gain dominion and victory when we speak His Word into the challenges of life.

# Supernatural Increase and Favor

## 1. Know Him and Call upon His Holy Name

The first image of intimacy in the Bible, at a human level, is in the Book of Genesis where it is written that Adam *"knew"* Eve. The Hebrew word is *yada*, which implies "an observation, recognition, and intimacy like the oneness of a consummated marriage." To know our God is to become one with Him, to surrender to Him in an act of love. He wants to live inside our natural bodies, as we are living in Him (see Acts 17:27-28).

God gave us His eternal name. He tells us in Exodus 3:13-15:

> *Then Moses said to God, "If I come to the people of Israel and say to them, 'The God of your fathers has sent me to you,' and they ask me, 'What is his*

*name?' what shall I say to them?" God said to Moses, "I AM WHO I AM." And he said, "Say this to the people of Israel, 'I AM has sent me to you.'" God also said to Moses, "Say this to the people of Israel, 'The LORD, the God of your fathers, the God of Abraham, the God of Isaac, and the God of Jacob, has sent me to you.' This is my name forever, and thus I am to be remembered throughout all generations."*

We know the actual name of God is so holy the Jews were careful to hide it so that no one could blaspheme His name, and they substituted the title: Lord. The prophets foretold that there was coming a Messiah, a Savior of the world, and anyone who called upon His name would be forgiven and would inherit eternal life (see Acts 4:12). His name is Jesus Christ (see Acts 4:10), Son of God, son of Mary, Root of Jesse. His name is the name that is above ALL other names (see Philippians 2:9-11 and Ephesians 1:21).

Christ is the Manna, the Bread of Life that our hearts long for (see John 6:33).

It is written, in Deuteronomy 4:29, that we are to continuously seek Him with a whole heart, and when we do, the promise is that we will find Him.

## 2. Imitate Jesus.

Jesus was obedient to the Father, even unto death. His eyes were always upon His Father in Heaven, and He did everything He was told to do. Jesus demonstrated that He was the Son of God through His utmost trust and obedience to the Father.

Jesus worshiped and prayed morning and night (see Psalm 113:3). He was always in the presence of His Father. He was in the Father, and the Father was in Him.

As believers in Christ, we are His body, and He is our Head. He is in us, and we are in Him. Jesus is living His resurrected life through us. He is our treasure, and we are His prize. We are the gift He has received for His suffering. The Father predestined us to conform to the image of His Son (see Romans 8:29).

We are to have the mind of Christ and to be filled with faith, hope, and love with all gentleness and humility (see Ephesians 4:1-2). We live a life of love and serve through the power and authority He gave us. We will also do the works He did (see John 4:12).

## 3. Be Ready for Christ's Return.

We are instructed to be ready for Christ's return by being full of His light. In Matthew 25:1-12, believers are portrayed as virgins going to meet their beloved Bridegroom in the middle of the night. They turn up the glow of their light to find their way to Him. The oil in the lamp speaks of the Holy Spirit. Our light increases as we yield to the Holy Spirit. Christ's return is eminent:

### Be prepared!
(see Luke 12:35-38 and 40,
2 Peter 3:13-14
and Revelation 16:15 and 19:7)

### Eagerly wait for His return!
(see Philippians 3:20 and Romans 8:19)

### Look forward to His glorious return!
(see Romans 8:18-19 and 2 Timothy 4:8)

Devout Jews pray toward Jerusalem, where God's Holy presence is still felt at the Western Wall (see Daniel 6:10 and Psalm 137:5). Jerusalem is God's throne (see Jeremiah 3:17) and Christ's footstool forever (see Ezekiel 43:7). Christ will return to the Mount of Olives (see Zechariah 14:4).

Jesus has set His eyes on Jerusalem (see Zechariah 1:16), so I am setting my eyes on Jerusalem as well. It is the greatest city on the earth and is called the City of Truth (see Zechariah 8:3, AMP), and the city of God's delight (see Isaiah 62:4). The eyes of the nations will be drawn to the righteousness of Zion when Christ reigns from Jerusalem.

### 4. Be a Blessing to Israel and the Jewish People

Experiencing the fullness of the Holy Spirit gave me a greater love for Israel and the Jewish people than I had ever known. Most early New Testament believers were Jewish, and they gave to the needs of those living in Jerusalem. The New Testament instructs the church: *"to the Jew first"* (Romans 1:16). This instruction has never been rescinded.

We have seen an increase of God's favor as we pursue the Jewish roots of our faith in Christ. We have seen an increase of God's favor as we bless Israel (see Genesis 12:3). Our hearts' cry to the Father is for the Jews to receive their Messiah, Christ (see Romans 11:12-27) and to be united with us in faith (see Ephesians 2:14-15 and 22, Romans 11:15 and Amos 9:11-13).

### 5. Publish His Magnificence and the Great and Mighty Works He Does

*Publish His glorious deeds among the nations;*
*tell everyone about the amazing things he does.*
*—Psalm 96:3*

The Scriptures are clear: we are to publish the magnificent deeds of the Lord. I have seen great and mighty deeds of the Lord in churches, yet absolutely nothing is said of it. It is as if church leadership has blinders on. Every revival began with a work of the Holy Spirit. I believe once the church starts publishing His great and mighty deeds and celebrating His goodness, we will receive greater favor from the Lord.

# Characteristics of the Messianic Age

BIBLICAL HISTORY IS SAID TO CONSIST of three ages, or periods, of time broadly defined as 1) The age of God's publishing His laws, 2) The Church age, which was birthed at Pentecost, and 3) The Messianic Age, when Christ rules and reigns on the earth.

By now you may be thinking, *Why is the Messianic Age important for Christians? And why is it part of this book?* This book is a testimony of my personally experiencing the great outpouring of the Holy Spirit, which I believe precedes the Messianic Age. I am sounding the trumpet for Heaven's purposes, to help Christians come into maturity in Him.

The Messianic Age has a great deal to do with your future. Everything you do in this life will affect your life in the future. God's current design and plan in this Church age is to bring believers in Christ into maturity. Jesus wants us to imitate Him and do the works that He did, and for everyone in the world to know, love, and surrender to Him.

The full spiritual equipping of the saints during the current Church age continues:

> *until we all attain to the unity of the faith and of the knowledge of the Son of God, to mature manhood, to the measure of the stature of the fullness of Christ.*

—Ephesians 4:13

New Testament references to the Messianic Age include Hebrews 6:5, speaking of those who had been enlightened and:

> *who have tasted the good word of God and the power of the age to come.* (NLT)

One day we will wake up to a new world order, with Christ seated in Jerusalem, Israel, and reigning over all the governments of the world. He has promised to return for His Bride, the Church. He has promised to return to the Mount of Olives in Jerusalem. He will enter through the Eastern Gate, when He comes to claim His Kingdom. He will have dominion over the entire world as a reward for His suffering. He has promised to bring with Him all the saints of all the ages from the ends of the earth and the ends of the Heaven, to share in His sovereign rule over the earth.

## GOD'S FUTURE DESIGN AND PLANS

The following scriptures are a sampling of God's future design and plans:

1. God launched His Kingdom on the earth with Jesus Christ's first coming (see Matthew 12:28, Mark 1:15, and Luke 4:43 and 11:20).
2. God's Kingdom includes the restoration of all things (see Jeremiah 30:9, Acts 3:21, 1 Corinthians 15:24 and Revelation 21:1-4).
3. There will be an epic outpouring of the Holy Spirit upon ALL people (see Joel 2:28-32, Isaiah 44:3 and 59:20-21 and Ezekiel 36:27).
4. God's Kingdom will be consummated by the return to earth of Jesus Christ (see Matthew 24:30-31, Mark 13:26-27 and Revelation 11:15 and 12:10).
5. There will be a universal acknowledgment of the Lord Jesus Christ (see Isaiah 2:2-3 and

19:23-25, Jeremiah 3:17, Zechariah 14:16, Micah 4:1-2 and Revelation 7:14).

6. Christ will rule and reign, bringing righteousness and justice to the earth (see Isaiah 9:6-7, 11:2-5, 32:1 and 32:16, Jeremiah 23:5-6 and 33:15-16, Psalm 72:2 and 12-13, 1 Corinthians 6:2, and Revelation 11:15, 19:15-16 and Revelation 20).

7. Christ will bring joy, peace, and security to Israel and the whole world (see Isaiah 2:4, 19:23-25, 32:17-18, 35:1, 35:10, and 65:20-23, Jeremiah 23:5-6 and 33:15-16, Ezekiel 34:25-29, Zechariah 9:9-10 and Micah 4:3-4).

# Declarations of the Glory Light

---

**LET THERE BE LIGHT:**

*Heavenly Father, we come to You in Jesus Christ and thank You for the light of Christ, which is good. We pray the spiritual light would be separated from the spiritual darkness in our nation. We ask for Your Holy Light to consume all spiritual darkness.* (Genesis 1:4, NLT)

**LIGHT TO SEE:**

*Heavenly Father, we come to You in Jesus Christ and declare You are the Fountain of Life and the Light by which we see. Give us eyes to see spiritual and natural manifestations, to align us with our heavenly assignments. We pray You would give us eyes to confirm that we have the true light and there be no darkness in us, our family, our community, our churches, or our nation.* (Psalm 36:9, NLT)

### LIGHT AND SALVATION:

*Father God, we come to You in Jesus Christ. We ask You to reveal the light and salvation that is in Jesus Christ to Israel. We ask You to reveal the light and salvation that is in Jesus Christ to all those living in America and every nation. We pray Your light and salvation would bring a worldwide spiritual revival to the Church and a great worldwide spiritual awakening.* (Psalm 27:1, NLT)

### LIGHT AND TRUTH:

*Father God, we come to You in Jesus Christ. Increase Your light and truth in us, for we desire to come into Your holy presence to worship You.* (Psalm 43)

### LIFE-GIVING LIGHT:

*Thank You, Father, for You have fulfilled Your promises, and we can and chose to live every day in Your life-giving light. May Your life-giving light bring physical and spiritual healing to the nations.* (Psalm 56:13, NLT)

### LIGHT OF WISDOM AND RIGHTEOUSNESS:

*Holy Father in Heaven, we come to You in Jesus Christ. May the light You have given us lift up wisdom and establish righteousness on the earth. May Your light expose what is hidden in the darkness and overtake it. May we walk in Your light and gaze upon Your glory.* (Proverbs 4:18, NLT)

### LIGHT LIKE FLAMES OF FIRE:

*Heavenly Father, we come to You in Jesus Christ. The winds are Your messengers, and flames of fire are Your servants. It is our pleasure and delight to serve You, Almighty God. As Your flames of fire, may we be stirred up by the wind of the Holy Spirit and be passionate and zealous unto good works.* (Psalm 104:4, NLT)

### WITNESSES OF THE LIGHT:

*Thank you Father, I am a witness to Your light, Jesus Christ, and I ask for open doors of opportunity to tell the world about Your light. May everyone who hears my testimony believe my testimony. Thank You for the light Christ gives to everyone. Thank You that the light of Christ overcomes and extinguishes all darkness.* (John 1:4-5 and Ephesians 5:8, NLT)

### GLORY LIGHT:

*Gracious Father in Heaven, we come to You in Jesus Christ. We declare that the light of Christ in us will be seen by all. Our lives will be radiant, and our faces will shine with Your glory and light.* (Luke 11:33, NLT)

## SECOND COMING LIGHT:

*Thank You, Father, You have scheduled a time and place for Christ Jesus to return to the earth. His return will be heralded by Your glorious and strikingly brilliant light that will flash from the east to the west, and every eye will see Him.* (Matthew 24:27, NLT)

# Recommended Reading

The Bible written by God through men inspired by
the Holy Ghost.

*Angels: Elect and Evil* by C. Fred Dickason, published by Moody Publishers, Chicago, Illinois:
1975.

*The Believer's Authority* by Kenneth E. Hagin, published by Faith Library Publications, Tulsa,
Oklahoma: 1985,

*Make Fear Bow* by Gary V. Whetstone, published by Whitaker House, New Kensington, Pennsylvania: 2002

*Seventy Reasons for Speaking in Tongues* by Dr. Bill
Hamon, published by Destiny Image Publishers, Shippensburg, Pennsylvania: 2012

*The Tongue: A Creative Force* by Charles Capps, published by Harrison House, Tulsa, Oklahoma: 1976.

*Unlocking the Hidden Mysteries of the Powers of the Age to Come* by Kevin Basconi and Michael Danforth, published by King of Glory Ministries International Publications, Moravian Falls, North Carolina: 2015.

*Your Pathway to Miracles* by Marilyn Hickey, published by Whitaker House, New Kensington, Pennsylvania: 2011.

## A Personal Invitation

If you have prayed to receive Christ and the baptism in the Holy Spirit, please let me know.

If you have been inspired by this book and have experienced God's supernatural power resulting in victory, we want to praise God with you.

Please contact me by email at:

TheAnointing2day@gmail.com.

# About the Author

Lucille Parkerson has a passion for leading believers into the deepest, most intimate relationship they can have with God and to experience the indescribable, holy, pure delight of daily hosting His Spirit. She and her husband are the parents of two grown children. They have been in Christian ministry for decades, serving in numerous church capacities, including Christian government, education, evangelism, discipleship, counseling, mentoring, intercessory and worship ministries, and social ministries, as well as serving international, national and community para-church organizations.

Lucille was instructed to write this book after receiving supernatural deliverance and healing, followed by a holy visitation of God, as written in Ephesians 3:19 (AMP):

*To know [practically, through personal expe-
rience] the love of Christ which far surpasses
[mere] knowledge [without experience], that you
may be filled up [throughout your being] to all
the fullness of God [so that you may have the
richest experience of God's presence in your lives,
completely filled and flooded with God Himself].*

She writes, "My body and the body of my Lov-
er, Jesus, my Redeemer were made one. His whole
person was living inside of my whole person, and
I was filled and flooded with the magnificent glory
light of Heaven."

May you find in these writings practical advice
on how to go to the highest level of a one-on-one
relationship with God. If so, you will experience
the pure joy, absolute euphoria, and great peace
discovered when all barriers of this planetary life
converge with God's supernatural realm.

Believers who seek and receive ALL Jesus died
to give them will come into maturity, operate under
His magnificent last-day's anointing, and advance
His Kingdom in the greatest magnitude since the
impact made by the first-century Church.

www.ingramcontent.com/pod-product-compliance
Lightning Source LLC
LaVergne TN
LVHW011202080426
835508LV00007B/551